A Review of Anglican Orders

The Problem and the Solution

by

George H. Tavard

A Michael Glazier Book
THE LITURGICAL PRESS
Collegeville, Minnesota

ABOUT THE AUTHOR

George H. Tavard, A.A., is internationally known as a Christian thinker whose theological and ecumenical work and writings have had a pioneering and salutary influence. Father Tavard writes with the surety of one who is intimately familiar with the sources and with the problems and nuances of contemporary theology. Among his many publications are *Theology of the Word; Woman in Christian Tradition; Images of Christ: An Inquiry in Christology; and A Theology For Ministry.*

A Michael Glazier Book

published by

THE LITURGICAL PRESS

1   2   3   4   5   6   7   8   9

Library of Congress Cataloging-in-Publication Data

Tavard, George H. (George Henry), 1922-
    A review of Anglican orders/by George H. Tavard.
        p. cm.—(Theology and life series; vol. 31)
    Includes bibliographical references.
    ISBN 0-8146-5800-8
    1. Anglican orders. 2. Catholic Church—Relations—Anglican Communion. 3. Anglican Communion—Relations—Catholic Church.
    I. Title. II. Series: Theology and life series; v. 31.
BX5178.T38   1990
262'.143—dc20
                                                          90-30918
                                                               CIP

Theo-
logy
&
Life

THEOLOGY AND LIFE SERIES

Volume 31

Contents

Foreword

The present book has been inspired by the official dialogue between Roman Catholics and Anglicans. The question was discussed informally in the context of ARCIC-I, of which I was a member. In the dialogue between Anglicans and Roman Catholics in the USA, the topic has been discussed officially. Having agreed to cooperate with one of the Anglican participants on a report regarding the current state of the question of Anglican orders, I made an extensive investigation of the matter. In fact, this was not the first time I approached the question. I had engaged in similar research during three years that I spent in England from 1949 to 1951. This research ended in my utter confusion regarding the extremely complicated aspects of the question in the sixteenth century.

Largely because of that, I suggested in 1971, tongue in cheek, that there be some sort of excommunication for anyone who would write more than ten pages on Anglican orders, unless that person said something really new.

I do not think I am now incurring this penalty. For something really new happened when Pope John Paul II opened the Vatican Archives for the period of the condemnation of Anglican ordinations by Pope Leo XIII. The most important documents from these Archives have now been published. And this allows anyone who cares to take a further look at the proceedings of 1895. Most of the present volume, however, concerns the earlier period, sixteenth to eighteenth century. My earlier confusion has been cleared up, at least to my satisfaction; and I believe I have something new to say regarding what some papal texts of the time really meant.

I trust that this study will be received in the irenic and ecumenical spirit in which it has been written.

Columbus, Ohio   George H. Tavard

Introduction:
The Problem

What Roman Catholic theology designates as the problem of Anglican orders was a creation of the past two centuries. It came to the surface as a question when, in the first half of the eighteenth century, several French theologians studied the history and the ritual of ordinations in the Church of England, and, in typical fashion, polemicized against one another.

The debate was reactivated in the nineteenth century. It was suggested in 1852, at the first diocesan synod after the restoration of the Roman Catholic hierarchy in England, that Anglican ordinations be solemnly declared null and void. The synod, however, did nothing of the kind: its members believed that these ordinations had already been declared invalid by several popes.

The contributions to the debate were mostly exercises in comparative theology and liturgiology. The central question concerned the rite of ordination in the Ordinal: is it capable of doing what is done by the corresponding rite in the Pontifical?

The Ordinal is the ritual of ordination appended to the Book of Common Prayer. There have been three successive forms of the Ordinal in the Church of England. Those of 1550 and 1552 were imposed on the Church by the government of Edward VI, chiefly under the theological influence of the archbishop of Canterbury, Thomas Cranmer, and through the political power of Protector Somerset. That of 1662 resulted from alterations that were introduced at the restoration of the monarchy, after the interregnum. During the Commonwealth, the government of Oliver Cromwell had abolished the episcopal form of the official Church, though it hesitated between a Presbyterian system of government by synods, preferred by the majority of Puritan divines (Presbyterians), and a Congregational polity, favored by the Independents and Cromwell himself.

The Pontifical is the liturgical book containing the rites of the various services that, according to the Catholic tradition, can be performed only by bishops. One could compare the sober ceremonies of the Ordinal with the more elaborate rites of the older Pontificals that were in use in England before the Reformation. These followed the Gallican model, that had slight differences from the Roman model. The main one was the rite of Sarum (old Salisbury). In 1542, king Henry VIII had selected the Sarum rite as the standard, thus eliminating others from regular usage.[1] One could also compare the Ordinal with the Roman Pontifical that was universally used in the Latin rite of the Catholic Church in the nineteenth century. Such a comparison usually reflected the centralizing mentality of the liturgical reformer, Dom Prosper Guéranger, who advocated the untraditional principle, one rite for one Church.

What had been a question turned into a problem when, urged from both sides, Leo XIII (pope from 1878 to 1903) examined the thesis of the validity of Anglican orders and found it wanting. Contrary to the expectations of many, he reached the negative conclusion: Anglican clergy who wish to enter the Roman Catholic Communion cannot be received as priests or deacons. They must be ordained unconditionally if they wish to function as clergy, the ordinations performed in the Church of England since the Reformation being invalid by Roman Catholic standards. The apostolic letter of Leo XIII, *Apostolicae curae,* was composed after a special advisory commission had discussed the matter. It was issued in 1896. A brief look at the structure of this document is useful at this time.

The letter may be divided into four sections.

(1) The pope begins with a survey of what are alleged to be relevant precedents. These are papal documents in which Julius III and Paul IV gave Cardinal Pole authority to deal with the canonical problems that were met when Queen Mary, at her accession after the death of her Protestant brother, Edward VI, desired the kingdom to be reconciled with the Holy See and the Catholic Church.

(2) In addition, two later cases are briefly looked at, in which, at the end of the seventeenth and the beginning of the eighteenth centuries, Roman authorities decided that two converts, ordained in the Church of England, needed to be ordained unconditionally if they were to function as priests in the Catholic Church.

(3) Next, the history and the text of the Ordinal are examined, special attention being paid to the "form" of episcopal consecration. The conclusion is reached that this form is insufficient for a valid consecration, and that the "intention" of those who used this rite in the sixteenth century was not the proper intention to "do what the Church does."

(4) The final conclusion is formulated: "We pronounce and declare that ordinations performed according to the Anglican rite have been and are *irritas . . . omninoque nullas*."[2] These Latin words are often translated: "absolutely null and utterly void." It is because Leo XIII considers the Ordinal ineffective that he concludes to the non-existence of the sacrament of orders in the Church of England. This is then followed by a pious exhortation to the Anglican clergy "to return to her [the Catholic Church's] bosom." The apostolic letter ends on a warning that any future attempt to invalidate the pope's conclusion on the ground of "subreption, obreption, defect in our intention, or any other defect," will be "ineffective and void" (*irritum et inane*).[3] Such a warning belongs to the customary language of the Roman curia. As is well known to scholars who have studied the history of the papacy, it ought not to be taken literally.

A great amount of scholarship was displayed on both sides of the debate, not least by the members of Leo XIII's commission. Much in the older Catholic books on this topic is still worth reading, although many of them suffer from naive acceptance of the Nag's Head story, that had been concocted in the polemical climate of the late Elizabethan controversies: the consecration of Matthew Parker as archbishop of Canterbury under Queen Elizabeth would have been highly farcical, taking place in a tavern without a proper rite! The legend had been put into print by Christopher Holywood in 1604, in a *De Investiganda vera ac visibili Christi ecclesia*. But it had been refuted time and time again. Even when they no longer accept the Nag's Head fable, the productions of the 1890's are often too intent on proving a thesis to be reliable sources of information.

The topic was researched again shortly before Vatican Council II, especially by Francis Clark (*Anglican Orders and Defect of Intention,* London: Longmans, Green & Co, 1956).[4] This new look at the question culminated with John Jay Hughes's pivotal investigation and critique of the Commission's work and of Leo's conclusion (*Absolutely Null and Utterly Void. An account of the 1896 Papal Condemnation of Anglican Orders,* Washington: Corpus Books, 1968, and *Stewards of the Lord. A Reappraisal of Anglican Orders,* London: Sheed and Ward, 1970). More recently, however, the opening of the Secret Archives of the Vatican for the end of the nineteenth century has brought to light documentation that was not hitherto available. Giuseppe Rambaldi, S.J., has pioneered this new research with the publication of several documents relating to the Commission of Leo XIII.[5]

The present volume is a review. As such, it does not replace the previous studies of the problem, whether made by Anglicans or by Roman Catholics. In fact, most of the points that will be stressed were available to Leo XIII's Commission. Yet I have put a special emphasis on the meaning of an expression that was used by the popes of the sixteenth century when they wrote to their legate in England, Cardinal Pole, and that was quite misunderstood in the nineteenth century: *haeresis hujusmodi* ("this kind of heresy"). This does not designate, as has been commonly assumed, Anglicanism as a whole, seen as a heretical movement. It is the "heresy of bigamy," that is, the marriage of priests. The sense of this expression in the papal documents throws a peculiar light on what actually was the central concern of the first pope who tried to facilitate the reconciliation with the Catholic Church of the English clergy who were schismatically ordained under Henry VIII and Edward VI. His attention was not focused on the effectiveness of the Anglican Ordinal. Rather, he was mesmerized by the ecclesiastical discipline of celibacy: what can and should be done with the deacons, priests, and bishops who acquired a wife, illegally under Henry VIII, legally under Edward VI, against the immemorial custom and the explicit canons of the

Catholic Church? This meaning of *haeresis hujusmodi,* however, was drowned for later times in the polemical quagmire that engulfed the whole question of Anglican ordinations. To what extent the popes' concern for clerical celibacy affected their judgment on Anglican orders is of course a moot point.

There were other problems. The papal legate in England had to reach agreement with the queen and her parliament regarding the ownership of the ecclesiastical goods stolen from the Church by Henry VIII, especially during the closing of the monasteries. New bishops, untainted by heresy, had to be selected to replace the bishops of Edward VI. Pope Julius III and his legate, Cardinal Pole, showed themselves remarkably lenient, installing as bishops several of those who had fallen into schism when they consented to the royal supremacy proclaimed by King Henry. But the popes had to draw the line somewhere. They drew it at two points. They would not accept heretical clergy unless these presented, along with due signs of regret, a clear profession of Catholic orthodoxy. And they would not tolerate the marriage of deacons, priests, and bishops.

The plan of the present survey has been suggested by the structure of *Apostolicae curae.*

Chapter 1 will examine the doctrines of Thomas Cranmer, archbishop of Canterbury, the man who was chiefly responsible for composing the Ordinal and who conspired with the ministers of Edward VI to impose it, along with the Book of Common Prayer, on the nation and the Church. This corresponds to the historical part of the third section of *Apostolicae curae.*

Chapter 2 will study the documents in which Pope Julius III sent instructions to Cardinal Reginald Pole, who, during the reign of Queen Mary and with her help, was entrusted with the task of restoring the Catholic Church in England.

Chapter 3 will make a similar study of the documents issued by pope Paul IV. These two chapters correspond to the first part of *Apostolicae curae.*

Chapter 4 will search for the origin of the claim that Anglican bishops are not bishops at all, in the polemics of Elizabethan times between Anglicans and Recusants.

Chapter 5 will look, somewhat briefly, at two cases that are brought forth by Leo XIII in support of his reading of the bulls of Julius III and Paul IV. These are decisions made in 1684 and 1704, under Popes Innocent XI and Clement XI. This corresponds to section three of Leo XIII's apostolic letter. Chapter 6 will describe the context and the work of Leo XIII's Commission.

Chapter 7 will examine the central argumentation of *Apostolicae curae,* that is, the alleged defect of "form and intention" in Anglican ordinations that was at the heart of Leo XIII's preoccupations. This corresponds in part to the theological dimension in the third section of *Apostolicae curae.*

Chapter 8 will present what has been called the contemporary "new context" for the evaluation of Anglican ordinations.

The conclusion will make suggestions for a possible solution of the remaining problem of the recognition of Anglican orders by the Catholic Church.

1

Thomas Cranmer

The most common argument against the validity of Anglican orders is that the Ordinals of 1550 and 1552, like the Books of Common Prayer of 1549 and 1552, were designed to exclude the sacrificial dimension of the eucharist and the correlative notion that priests are ordained to offer the sacrifice of the mass for the quick and the dead. In support of this interpretation of the liturgical reforms of the Church of England under Edward VI, one cites the fact that Archbishop Cranmer was staunchly opposed to a sacerdotal conception of the presbyterate. It will therefore be useful at this point to take a look at the theology of Thomas Cranmer. In composing the Book of Common Prayer and the Ordinal, Cranmer drew on ideas suggested by Martin Bucer (1491-1551) and Peter Martyr Vermigli (1500-1562), both of them continental reformers who were in England at the time. He was of course assisted in his work by others, notably by Nicholas Ridley (c.1500-1555), bishop of Rochester in 1547, then of London in 1550, and by Richard Cox (1500-1581), who was to become bishop of Ely in 1559.[1]

Archbishop Cranmer

Thomas Cranmer (1489-1555) was a scholar at Cambridge. He had married and been widowed early. Ordained in 1523, his suggestions for solving the problem of King Henry's divorce from his childless queen, Catherine of Aragon, brought him to the king's attention in 1528. Henry appointed him to the universities' commission that gave an official advice in favor of the divorce. He soon became archdeacon of Taunton and one of the king's chaplains. He led royal embassies to Rome and to the Holy Roman Germanic Empire when Henry tried to marshal diplomacy to force the hand of the pope in the matter of the divorce. During this last mission he entered a clandestine and illegal marriage with Margaret, a niece of the Nuremberg reformer, Andreas Osiander (1498-1552). He was appointed to the see of Canterbury, being consecrated a bishop on March 30, 1533. Since Henry was staunchly opposed to clerical marriage, Cranmer's wife had to lead a hidden existence in the recesses of Lambeth palace. At the king's request, Cranmer had received the proper papal bull confirming Cranmer's election and authorizing his consecration. The ceremony included an oath of allegiance to papal authority, which Cranmer did take. Yet he had previously signed a secret document to the effect that he did not intend to commit himself by such an oath! In the following May, as archbishop, Cranmer pronounced Henry's marriage to Catherine null and void, thus opening the way to the legalization of the king's marriage to Ann Boleyn.

Henceforth the archbishop led a double life. On the one hand he tried to reform the Church of England in a decidedly Protestant direction. In this he met the opposition of the king and of a powerful clerical party, led by the bishop of Winchester, Stephen Gardiner (c.1583-1555). Cranmer welcomed the royal supremacy, which had grown through a series of acts of Parliament, to be crowned in 1534, the king being now "supreme head of the Church in England." But he failed in his attempt to reform the liturgy, as the king did not let him introduce more than a litany in English. On the other hand, Cranmer superficially and officially agreed with Henry's conservative doctrinal stance regarding the sacraments. Meanwhile, he remained the king's tool for such unsavory acts as the annulment of the king's marriage to Anne Boleyn, in 1536, and the spoliation and suppression of the monasteries.

When Henry died on January 28, 1547, Thomas Cranmer was prepared to encourage the Protestant convictions of the young Edward VI, and he became the main architect of the reform of religion. He eagerly supported the legalization of clerical marriage. The new liturgy was his work. When Edward died, however, on July 6, 1553, Cranmer made a major political mistake. He acquiesced, though perhaps reluctantly, to the duke of Northumberland's attempt to give the crown to a Protestant queen, the young Lady Jane Grey (1537-1554), who was a grand-daughter of Henry VIII's younger sister, Mary. The conquest of the throne by Henry's elder daughter, the Princess Mary, spelt the end of his power.

Cranmer's Eucharistic Doctrines

Cranmer's doctrines concerning the eucharist are developed at great length in his bitter polemic with Stephen Gardiner. A relatively short piece, *Defense of the True and Catholic Doctrine of the Sacrament of the Body and Blood of Christ,* was published by Cranmer in 1550, that is, as soon as, by King Henry's death, the archbishop was able to escape the king's protection of sacramental orthodoxy.[2] Stephen Gardiner made a sharp critique of it, from the standpoint of the tradition, in *An Explication and Assertion of the True Catholic Faith touching the Most Blessed Sacrament of the Altar.* Cranmer's rebuke of Gardiner, who by this time had been deprived of his see and removed to the Tower, is entitled, *Answer to a Crafty and Sophistical Cavillation devised by Stephen Gardiner against the True and Godly Doctrine of the Most Holy Sacrament of the Body and Blood of Our Savior Jesus Christ.* It is Cranmer's major writing. Published in 1551, it departs from standard Catholic teaching on the sacrament of the Lord's Supper. As was customary in the theological polemics of the sixteenth century, Cranmer quotes his adversary at length before refuting him point by point. After a general discussion of the sacrament (book I), Cranmer seeks to refute Gardiner's position on the sacramental presence (bk II, against Gardiner's book III), the reception of the body and blood of Christ (bk III, against Gardiner's book IV), transubstantiation (bk IV, refuting Gardiner's book II), and the eucharist as sacrifice (bk V).

Two interpretations of Cranmer's eucharistic theology have been proposed. Many authors, particularly Roman Catholic ones, see it as coming straight from Calvin or Zwingli, whose doctrines Cranmer knew from his own readings and from his friendship with continental divines. Cranmer's conception of the sacramental presence by faith is in fact more radical than that of the French reformer. It owes more to Zwingli than to Calvin. Some other authors, chiefly Anglicans, esteem that Cranmer was less a reformer of current doctrines concerning the holy eucharist than a rediscoverer of an older doctrine that had been discarded in the course of the Middle Ages. This was the symbolic sacramentalism of Berengarius (c.999-1088), which itself was based on that of Paschasius Radbertus (c.785-c.860), and ultimately on the symbolic strain in St. Augustine's sacramental theology.[3]

Without going into details that are not necessary at this point, I would judge that the milder interpretation does not do justice to the minimalism of the definition that Cranmer included in his project for a *Reformatio legum ecclesiasticarum,* of 1552: the eucharist is "a sacrament in which they who sit as guests at the Lord's Holy Table eat bread and drink wine!"[4] Besides, most of Cranmer's critique is directed against a doctrine that is not Catholic at all, namely, that the body of Christ is quantitatively present on the altar. In other words, Cranmer never really understood the Catholic doctrine and its explanation by the scholastics. One may think, however, that his view of the eucharist evolved. It passed through several steps and stages.

The Curve of Cranmer's Theology

Cranmer's theology is based on his endorsement of justification by faith, that was for a time at the center of debates between the followers and the opponents of Martin Luther. But Cranmer's understanding of justification is closer to Calvin than to Luther. "Perfect faith," he writes, "is nothing else than an assured trust and confidence in God's mercy."[5] This trust is founded in "the gracious and benign promises of God by the mediation of Christ," that are known by the Scriptures. It results in God's acceptance of our imperfect works as though they were perfect: "By the merit and benefit of Christ, we being sorry that we cannot do all things no more exquisitely and duly, all our works shall be accepted and taken of God as most exquisite, pure, and perfect." Here, as in the homilies on Faith and on Good Works that are included in the *Book of Homilies,* there is a subtle shift from Luther's stress on God's action through Christ in the process of justifying the sinner, to what will be the Puritans' emphasis on the works of the saints.[6]

The second step in the evolution of Cranmer's theology was taken when he drew the implications of his view of justification for the doctrine of the sacraments. The works that, although imperfect in themselves, God accepts as perfect, are done for the neighbor's sake, in the charity that is inseparable from true faith. Put in these terms, a sacrament cannot be a work. As is stated in *Questions put concerning some Abuses of the Mass* (1547), "the sacrament of the altar was not instituted to be received by one man for another, but to be received by every man for himself."[7] In other words, the spiritual marrow of the sacrament is not found in outward actions; it lies in memory, namely, in the remembrance of that "very true sacrifice and immolation which was made upon the cross."

In the third step of his theological thinking, Thomas Cranmer related his conclusions concerning the sacraments to Calvin's christological principle, that is usually referred to as the *extra Calvinisticum*: the divinity of Christ is both in the body assumed at the Incarnation, and outside this body, for it pervades the universe by virtue of the divine immensity.[8] As applied to the eucharist, this principle justified Cranmer's contention, in his *Answer to Gardiner,* that "Christ (as concerning his body and manhood) is in heaven, and shall there continue until he come down at the last judgment."[9] Being in heaven, his body and blood cannot be in the sacrament on earth! Indeed, Cranmer went far beyond this, when he completely disconnected the sacramental body and blood of Christ from the Incarnation: "We say that they [the fathers and prophets of the Old Testament] did eat his body and drink his blood, although he was not yet born nor incarnated."[10]

Finally, Cranmer logically rejected all doctrines and theologies according to which there is something in the sacrament that is actually done by the Church through the ministry of priests. He therefore denied the real presence, transubstantiation, and the offering or sacrifice.

Summing up Cranmer's doctrines, one may say the following. The heart of his religious belief undoubtedly lies in the doctrine of justification by faith. His view of the sacrament is a consequence and application of it. The royal supremacy will simply be the chief tool and instrument through which he will try to make justification by faith, as he understood it, supreme in all things in the Church of England. The reform of the liturgy will be his preferred catechetical channel to bring it down to the level of the people.

All this, however, came out slowly onto the public stage. For Cranmer could not act beyond what was tolerable to Henry VIII. Further, he himself endorsed, willy nilly, Catholic formulations that were dear to the king. Several Latin articles were drawn up by Cranmer, probably for discussion with a team of Lutheran divines who came to London in 1538. They contain the following statement, that is in exact contradiction to what Cranmer actually believed:

> Concerning the eucharist, we firmly believe and teach that in the sacrament of the body and blood of the Lord there are substantially and really present the body and blood of Christ under the species of bread and wine . . .[11]

When Cranmer brought out the first Book of Common Prayer, in 1549, he thought he had eliminated from the Church's prayer all the points of sacramental theology that he now rejected. He was therefore surprised when Stephen Gardiner interpreted it in the sense of transubstantiation or the real presence, two formulae which the bishop of Winchester identified as one doctrine.[12] Cranmer therefore revised the book in a more radical direction. He had it reissued in a new form on April 6, 1552. This time, the formulations that had received Gardiner's approval were systematically altered or eliminated. As some other bishops, notably John Hooper (d. 1555), bishop of Gloucester, were more extreme than Cranmer in their opposition to vestments and ceremonies, the king's privy council wanted to placate them. It therefore introduced a warning not to interpret holy communion in the sense of the real presence of the body and blood of Christ. This is the so-called "black rubric":

> . . .it is not meant thereby that any adoration is done, or ought to be done, either unto the sacramental bread or wine there bodily received, nor to any real and essential presence there being of Christ's natural flesh and blood. For as concerning the sacramental bread and wine, they remain still in their very natural substances, and therefore may not be adored, for that were idolatry to be abhorred of all faithful Christians. And as concerning the natural body and blood of our Saviour Christ, they are in heaven and not here. For it is against the truth of Christ's true natural body, to be in more places than one at the same time.[13]

The insertion of this rubric was not Cranmer's doing. Yet it was entirely consistent with his theology. In any case, the alterations introduced into the Book of Common Prayer between 1549 and 1552 did not affect the Ordinal: this remained the same, with minor differences regarding the vestments to be worn and the porrection of the instruments.

Cranmer's View of Episcopacy

It was the conflict with Gardiner that occasioned the archbishop's main theological writings. But these do not explain his views of episcopacy. In fact, his understanding of the priesthood and the episcopate is clearly set forth in a paper in Latin, entitled, *De ordine et ministerio sacerdotum et episcoporum.* The date is uncertain, but one may gather from its contents regarding the king's authority in matters spiritual that it was composed under Henry VIII, and therefore before Thomas Cranmer began the liturgical reforms of the reign of Edward VI.

The basic principle is entirely traditional:

> Scripture openly teaches that the order and ministry of priests (*sacerdotum*) and bishops was not instituted by human authority, but divinely. It teaches that Jesus Christ, our Lord and Savior, instituted in the Church certain ministers of his word as his legates and the dispensers of the mysteries of God (as Paul calls them), who not only must

feed the flock with the good doctrine of Christ, but also . . .
lead all to perfect knowledge, love, and fear of God as well
as to sincere love of neighbor, who must consecrate the
body and blood of Christ in the sacrament of the altar . . .
and the power, function, and ministration of these ministers
is necessary to the Church as long as we fight on this earth
against the flesh, the world, and Satan, and on no occasion
must it be abolished . . .[14]

Cranmer gives three reasons for the necessity of the ministry
of priests and bishops: it is God's precept; it is the only means
of reconciliation with Christ and reception of the Holy Spirit;
it was given by Christ to the apostles as the way to "administer
God's word and sacraments."[15]

It follows that bishops must be very careful to ordain the
right persons. Priests and bishops must fight erroneous doctrine, superstition, idolatry. They must protect and promote
the glory of God and true piety. While indeed they have received from Christ the "power to bind and to excommunicate,"
they must not use corporal violence on those whom they excommunicate. Furthermore, they must organize the life of the
Church, make decisions regarding the times of public prayer
and liturgical services, the rites and ceremonies to be followed
in the administration of the sacraments and the celebration of
public prayer.

The rest of the document is devoted to the thesis that bishops
are, by divine institution, equal. All differences of "powers and
jurisdictions" between "patriarchs, primates, archbishops and
metropolitans" are of human origin. As to the authority that is
claimed by the Roman pontiffs, it is "vain and fictitious," it
"comes neither from God in the sacred books, nor from the
holy fathers in the ancient general councils or from the consent of the Catholic Church."[16]

The Royal Supremacy

If the doctrine of justification by faith and the sacramen-
tarian theology of Zwingli may be identified as the main ingre-
dients in Cranmer's doctrinal reforms, the central piece of his

organization of the Church is the royal supremacy. Instead of papal authority, "God has instituted and ordered that the authority of Christian kings and princes for the governance of the people be total and supreme, and that it dominate and exceed all other powers and offices."[17] For "to the kings as the supreme heads of the public good (*reipublicae*) God has committed the care and governance of all the people who live in their kingdoms and dominion, without any exception." Christian princes must therefore "protect and defend Christian doctrine, and abolish abuses, heresies, and idolatry."

Clearly, Thomas Cranmer's view of authority in the Church amounts to a kind of caesaro-papism. The supreme authority for organization and the implementation of decisions lies in the king. Yet bishops and priests also have their own authority by ordination. They are responsible for preaching the word and administering the sacraments, and thereby for determining what are the proper rites and ceremonies. There are thus two seats of spiritual authority, which is temporal in the king or prince, and ecclesial in the priests and bishops. However, the possibility of a conflict between these two seats of authority is not considered, nor is the relationship of priests and bishops clarified. There is no suggestion at this point that Cranmer wishes to alter the current rituals, and still less that his conception of the priesthood and the episcopate is at variance from that of the Catholic Church at large.

Priest and Sacrifice

Cranmer does not seem to have ever wavered from the concepts of priesthood and episcopacy that he formulated in the last years of Henry VIII. The only point on which his views were forced to evolve by circumstances relates to his Erastianism. In the Latin articles of 1538, the doctrine is stated as follows:

> Concerning the Church's ministers we teach that no one must teach or administer the sacraments publicly, unless he has been properly called (*rite vocatus*), and indeed by those with whom the right to call and to admit is located according

to the word of God and the laws and customs of each given region.[18]

Here, the hand is extended to the Lutherans of Germany, whose ordinations have not been made by bishops. Cranmer evidently knew that consecration by bishops is not taught in Holy Scripture. It is a creation of the Church's early tradition. Local custom, enforced by the prince, determines in each place the proper rite of ordination for all ranks of the ministry, so that each minister will be *rite vocatus.* Hence there are places where ordination may be done by priests rather than by bishops. Strictly speaking, ordination is not even necessary. Yet there is no suggestion in Cranmer's writings that the rite of ordination ought to depend on the determination of disputed points in eucharistic doctrine.

Indeed, Cranmer denies that the eucharist may be offered like a sacrifice. If it is called a sacrifice, this is only because "it is a memory and representation of that very true sacrifice and immolation which before was made upon the cross."[19] That this formula has a perfectly traditional Catholic sense escaped Cranmer, for whom the papist teaching has always been that "Christ is offered and sacrificed by the priest and the people." But his theological theories, and the ensuing misreading of the Catholic doctrine, were not responsible for the rites of ordination that Cranmer chose in 1550 and 1552.

Reform of Ordination

Cranmer intended the Ordinal to be the instrument through which, in England, the threefold order of the ministry would be transmitted and maintained. In the words of the preface to the Ordinal,

> It is evident unto all men, diligently reading Holy Scriptures and ancient Authors, that from the Apostles' time there have been three Orders of Ministers in Christ's Church, Bishops, Priests, and Deacons . . . And therefore, to the intent that these Orders may be continued, and reverently used and esteemed in this Church, no man shall be ac-

counted to be lawful Bishop, Priest, or Deacon, in this Church, or suffered to execute any of the said Functions, except he be called, tried, examined, and admitted thereunto, according to the Form hereafter following, or hath had Episcopal consecration or Ordination.[20]

The Ordinal abolished the minor orders and the subdiaconate. In the ordination of deacons it omitted the invocation of saints; added the royal supremacy oath, with the rejection of papal authority; kept the imposition of hands, but replaced the declaration, "Receive the Holy Spirit for strength . . .," with the banal formula, "Take thou authority to execute the office of a deacon in the Church committed to thee"; omitted the prayer for God's grace, the preface, the vesting; replaced the presentation of the liturgical Book of the Gospels (*Evangeliarium*) with a presentation of the New Testament. The task of a deacon is mentioned explicitly in the prayers and the scriptural readings.

In the ordination of a priest, the exhortation is purged of references to the celebration of the mass and the consecration of the eucharist. The laying on of hands is retained. The preface is replaced by a new blessing: "Receive the Holy Ghost for the office and work of a priest in the Church of God, now committed unto thee by the imposition of our hands . . . Whose sins . . . Be thou a faithful dispenser of the word of God and of his holy sacraments . . ." There is no vesting, no anointing. The porrection of the instruments, preserved in 1550, is reduced in 1552 to the presentation of a Bible. The service ends with a collect, addressed to "Almighty God, giver of all good things, who by the Holy Spirit hast appointed divers orders of ministers in thy Church . . ."

In the ordination of a bishop, the same royal supremacy oath is taken as in the ordination of a deacon. A promise of "due reverence and obedience" to the archbishop is added, replacing the promise of obedience to the pope. The prayers make no mention of consecration, ordination, sacrifice, or "high priesthood." It is clear, and generally unquestioned, that Thomas Cranmer embodied his own conception of orders and priesthood in the rite.

The Catholic Restoration

One can imagine Cranmer's dismay and dilemma when, by virtue of the royal supremacy, Queen Mary decided to restore, along with papal authority, the clerical discipline of celibacy and the eucharistic doctrines of Stephen Gardiner, that Cranmer had systematially fought. In the end, Cranmer was the victim of the inconsistency of his own thinking, as his theological convictions concerning the sacrament ran afoul of his political support of the royal supremacy. His theological convictions finally won, at the cost of his life. Yet he was also the victim of Pope Paul IV's unbending temperament and policy. Paul IV was both an ardent reformer and a strict enforcer of orthodoxy. As Cardinal Carafa he had, under Paul III, in 1542, reshaped the Roman Inquisition to make it more effective. Carafa was no respecter of persons. The Venetian lay cardinal Gasparo Contarini (1483-1542) had been Carafa's moderate colleague in Paul III's special commission for Church reform, the *Consilium de emendenda ecclesia.* Yet he was suspected of doctrinal error when, at the Regensburg colloquy (April-July 1541), he reached agreement with Philip Melanchthon on a number of controverted topics. Contarini died on the way to Rome, where he had been called to explain his endorsement of the *Regensburg Book.*[21] When the general vicar of the Capuchins, Bernardino Ochino (1487-1564), was likewise summoned to Rome in 1542 from central and northern Italy, to explain his preaching about justification by faith, he was so scared of Carafa that he fled to Geneva.

The Condemnation of Cranmer

Twice, Pope Clement VII had threatened to excommunicate Henry VIII, but the bulls that were drawn up to that effect were never in fact promulgated. Neither Paul IV nor Pius V (who will excommunicate Elizabeth) shared Clement's scruples and hesitancies. It was in keeping with Paul IV's systematic policy of reconquest, and in the logic of his attempt to strengthen the Church by reinforcing its orthodoxy, that he should personally attack the archbishop of Canterbury. At the consistory of December 4, 1555, the pope proceeded to the degradation of Thomas Cranmer. He reviewed the case of the king and queen of England versus Thomas Cranmer, "former archbishop of Canterbury," whom they had denounced as being guilty "of the crime of heresy and of other excesses, censures, and pains". In particular, Paul IV proclaimed:

> . . . we pronounce, judge, decide, and declare:
> that the said Thomas, then archbishop of Canterbury,— oblivious of the salvation of his soul,—judging and teaching against the rules and dogmas of the Church and of the holy Fathers, as also against the traditions of the Apostolic Roman Church and of the holy Councils, and against the customary rites of the Christian religion as hitherto [received] in the Church, especially concerning the sacraments of the body and blood of our Lord Jesus Christ and of holy Orders, otherwise than as Holy Mother Church preaches and observes,—denying the primacy and authority of the Holy Apostolic See and of the Supreme Pontiff,—believing, following, writing, printing, and publishing, . . . defending, renovating the heresy that was abjured by the deacon Berengar of Angers,—and even in front of our subdelegate . . . pertinaciously asserting, . . . among others, the condemned, false, and heretical dogmas of the heretics Wycliff and Martin Luther, . . . —and persevering in this his obstinacy,
>
> has fallen into and incurred the statutory pain . . . of excommunication . . .
>
> and therefore [we declare] this Thomas excommunicated and anathematized, deprived of the said archbishopric of Canterbury and of other prelacies, dignities, offices, benefices, pensions, rights, privileges, possessions, . . .
>
> to be turned over to the Secular Tribunal, his possessions confiscated, . . .
>
> and we condemn the same Thomas to perpetual silence concerning all these matters . . .[22]

As soon as the consistory was over, Paul IV regarded the

see of Canterbury as vacant by virtue of the deposition of Cranmer. He proceeded to name a successor. In the consistory of December 11, 1555, Pole was made "administrator of the Church of Canterbury," and promoted to the rank of cardinal-priest. The excommunication of Cranmer was made public a few days later, on December 14, 1555, in the bull, *Dudum per litteras vestras*. Cranmer's deposition and degradation naturally followed his excommunication. And it is certain that the turning over to the Secular Tribunal (*Saecularis Curia*) was an open invitation to the secular authorities in England to bring Cranmer to the stake and burn him.

Cranmer had in fact been placed under a loose form of house-arrest at Lambeth Palace in August 1553. In September, after he had publicly attacked the Catholic eucharistic doctrines, he was sent to the Tower. In March of 1554, he was forced to take part, along with Ridley and Hugh Latimer (c.1483-1555), bishop of Worcester, in a theological debate at Oxford, in the presence of Bishop Thirlby who acted as Pole's delegate. The archbishop defended the Edwardine reformation and bitterly attacked the Catholic eucharistic doctrine.

After their own separate trials, Ridley and Latimer were found guilty of heresy on October 1, 1554; they were degraded on the 14th, and burnt at Oxford on October 15. Cranmer was formally tried for heresy on September 12 and 13, 1555, before James Brookes (1520-1560), the new bishop of Gloucester, who, as papal subdelegate, presided over the tribunal. Yet, perhaps because of personal scruples on the part of Reginald Pole, who was evidently destined to become the next archbishop of Canterbury, the queen had done nothing to bring about Cranmer's death. The way, however, had now been indicated by the pope. Cranmer's degradation took place on February 14, 1556, before two bishops who went back respectively to King Henry's reign and to the first years of King Edward. Unlike Cranmer, however, they had opted for Catholic orthodoxy at Queen Mary's accession. They were Edmund Bonner (c.1500-1569), of London, ordained under Henry in 1540, and Thomas Thirlby (c.1506-1570), of Ely, who had been ordained under Edward, on April 1, 1550, with the old Pontifical. On March 21, 1556, after his last minute recantations, Cranmer was burnt at Oxford.

Conclusion

Paul IV's harassment of Thomas Cranmer is relevant to the investigation of Anglican Orders. Indeed, the pope's indictment of the archbishop finds fault with his teaching on the eucharist and the sacrament of orders and with his departure from the customary rite of the Church. Yet Paul IV nowhere accuses him of promoting false bishops and false priests to their respective offices. Like the disputation at Oxford before bishop Heath, the interrogations at Cranmer's trial brought out his eucharistic heresies. The Ordinal was in question insofar as it was not a rite approved by Rome or in use in the universal Church. But it was not in question as to its capacity, when used by the right persons, to make authentic priests.

In order more fully to assess the situation in regard to Anglican Orders, especially the episcopate, at the end of Queen Mary's reign, one needs to look carefully at the position of Popes Julius III and Paul IV regarding the ordinations performed in the period of schism.

Chapter 2

Julius III

The first bishop of Rome who had to face the question of the priesthood during the first English reformation (before the reign of Mary Tudor) was Julius III (pope in 1550; d. 1555). One main document describes his attitude to orders received and ordinations performed during the schism of Henry VIII and Edward VI. This is *Dudum cum charissima,* of March 8, 1554. A previous bull, *Si ullo unquam tempore* (August 5, 1553), in which Pope Julius designates Cardinal Reginal Pole as his legate in England, is sometimes alleged to refer to orders. But it makes no mention of such a question. Two assumptions have been generally made concerning these documents and those of Paul IV. First, it has been taken for granted that they reflect a coherent doctrine, even if this doctrine is not fully formulated in them. Second, it has been assumed that the popes gave clear instructions to their legate in England on what principles should be applied to the question of admitting Ordinal-ordained priests to the Catholic ministry. These assumptions were made by Leo XIII, when he referred to the instructions given by Julius III and Paul IV to Cardinal Pole, the papal legate in England.

Whether such assumptions should be made is highly questionable. Firstly, one cannot assume that the judgment of Julius III and that of Paul IV were identical. The former saw the accession of a Catholic queen to the throne of England. Every hope was then permitted for the return of the English nation to Catholic unity. The latter saw the situation deteriorate in the last years of Queen Mary's reign, and the accession of her sister Elizabeth, who was determined to reject papal authority and restore the royal supremacy. Through a subtle mixture of cajoling and threatening, Elizabeth imposed a moderate reforming platform on the Church of England while refusing to "make for herself a window into men's souls."[1] The hope of a Catholic England was then fading fast. The different circumstances of the two pontificates may well have inspired diverse attitudes regarding the value of the Ordinal.

Secondly, each of the papal documents was prompted by a particular set of questions arising out of specific situations. The answer may well have been, by the nature of the case, an *ad hoc* decision, applicable only to similar cases. It would therefore be a mistake to look for a full theology of orders and ordination in such documents. At the most, one may infer from them some elements for such a theology, but this theology is not necessarily identical with that of our own contemporary theologians and magisterium. Looking at the sixteenth century, one should assess the position of the various actors in the drama of the Reformation in the light of the theology and doctrine of the period, not in that of later centuries. Imposing our contemporary standards on texts and decisions of the past can only lead to anachronistic conclusions that will be of little historical and theological value.

The Accession of Mary Tudor

Mary acceded to the throne in July of 1553, after the collapse of the privy council's attempt to give the crown to her Protestant cousin, Lady Jane Grey. On August 18, the queen made her intentions known in matters of religion. She

> could not now hide that religion, which God and the world knoweth she hath ever professed from her infancy hitherto; which her majesty is minded to observe and maintain for herself by God's grace during her time, so doth her highness much desire, and would be glad, the same were of all her subjects quietly and charitably entertained.[2]

Nevertheless, the queen did not intend "to compel any her said subject thereunto, until such time as further order, by common assent, may be taken therein." In the meantime, all must "live together in quiet sort and Christian charity, leaving those newfound devilish terms of papist and heretick, and such like . . ." Those who will trouble the peace shall be punished accordingly. The common assent envisaged by the queen is evidently the concurrence of parliament in favor of the restoration of the old religion, whenever parliament is able to meet.

A spectacular breach of the peace was not long in coming, from a quarter that must have shocked the queen. The duke of Northumberland, now at the Tower, having renounced Protestantism, Archbishop Thomas Cranmer, who was still undisturbed at Lambeth palace despite his endorsement of Jane Grey, launched an open challenge. He solemnly announced in public that he was prepared to demonstrate that "the Mass in many things not only has no foundation of Christ's Apostles nor the Primitive church, but also is manifestly contrary to the same, and containeth many horrid abuses."[3] The archbishop was promptly removed to the Tower.

The queen was crowned on September 26. In November the House of Commons, after a week's debate, passed a new law concerning the establishment of religion: after December 20, the only liturgy allowed in England would be that which was legal in the last year of Henry VIII. Thus was the old religion restored in principle through parliament, by virtue of the queen's royal supremacy. Yet, given the previous rejection of papal authority by parliament and convocation and the proclamation of the royal supremacy, the kingdom as a whole still lay in schism. It needed an official reconciliation with the Holy See. This was to come one year later, on November 30, 1554, when Cardinal Pole, as papal legate, would absolve the kingdom. In the meantime, many problems had to be solved rapidly if the ordinary people in the land were to benefit from the ministry of priests in good standing.

The Papal Legate

Knowing Mary's dispositions toward the Catholic faith and

her hostility to the Reformation, Rome acted quickly in 1553. No sooner had the news of Edwards VI's death reached the city of Rome, than Pope Julius III, in the brief *Allato nobis nuntio,* of August 2, 1553, enquired from Cardinal Pole what should now be done to restore "the pious cult of religion and the observance of the holy laws" in England, "what should be hoped for, what should be attempted, what should be done or organized by us, or in what other way."[4] Pole was asked whether he should not now be sent as papal legate on a visit to the emperor and to the king of France. Three days later, Pole's mission was determined. On August 5 he was designated papal legate in England for the reconciliation of the kingdom (bull *Si ullo unquam tempore*). Pole, Julius III declares in this bull, has been "chosen as our legate, and that of the apostolic see, to Queen Mary and to the entire kingdom of England."[5] The powers of the legate are not itemized. But the pope exhorts him "to neglect nothing by which, with God's help, the fortunate fruit of his legation may be obtained, in consoling those who have fallen into error and bringing [them] back to the grace of God and the communion of his Holy Catholic Church."

The extent of Pole's authority was defined in principle in the bull, *Post nuntium nobis,* of August 6. The purpose of Pole's mission was, (1) to bring the queen the Holy See's congratulations and best wishes, (2) to use his own "virtue, piety, wisdom, doctrine, and authority, in order to bring back the troubled state of religion to the discipline of the Fathers."[6] As to the concrete measures to be taken, the pope leaves them entirely to his discretion:

> As to what it is proper to do, you need not be admonished by us, for you know about these things as much as we do and more than all others. What depends on us we have done promptly and eagerly in order to equip your circumspection with the most ample faculties from us and from this Apostolic See, with which to be able to console those who fell into error, and to restore them to God's grace and in the communion of his Holy Catholic Church, as will be explained at greater length in the letters to be given under our seal, that we will send you soon.

On the same day, August 6, the queen was notified of Pole's legation (*Posteaquam renuntiatum nobis*).

Reginald Pole

Reginald Pole (1500-1559), a descendant of the Plantagenets, belonged to one of the great families of England and was related to the Tudors. After attending Oxford University, Pole had traveled to Padua, where he had pursued his studies. In 1525 he had made a brief sojourn in Rome. He had returned to England in 1527. In 1529 he went to Paris for further studies at the university. Suddenly, Henry named him his ambassador, for the purpose of persuading the Sorbonne to approve his projected divorce. Again in England in 1530, Pole had a stormy meeting with the king on the matter of the divorce. Yet Henry let him go abroad in 1532: Pole went to southern France, and then to Venice. In 1535, when Henry was gathering opinions on the legality of his first marriage, and on the nature of the papal supremacy in matters spiritual, Pole, instead of giving the short answer that was requested, started a long manuscript, that he eventually sent to the king. Invited, on June 14, 1536, to return to England to explain himself further, Pole declined in a letter of July 25. His writing against the Henrician schism was not destined for publication. Yet it was brought out in Rome, without Pole's authorization, around 1539, under the title, *Pro ecclesiasticae unitatis defensio.*[7] It was largely because of this book that Pole's mother, the countess of Salisbury, was, on Henry's orders, executed for treason on May 27, 1541.

In the meantime, Pole was made a cardinal-deacon on December 23, 1536, and he was, on that occasion, reluctantly persuaded to receive the diaconate. He was named to the commission on the Reform of the Church, the *Consilium de emendanda ecclesia,* that gave its report in 1537. Hoping to obtain a reconciliation with Henry VIII, Paul III, on February 15, 1537, named Pole papal legate in England, but the legate and his retinue went only as far as Flanders and did not cross the channel. Soon, Pole was one of the papal legates who presided over the first sessions of the Council of Trent, beginning in 1542. A retiring scholar, with no worldly ambition, the

English cardinal was a man of the new learning that marked the Renaissance, eager to spend his life in peace and study. He was a friend of Cardinal Gasparo Contarini and of the distinguished lady, Vittoria Colonna (1494-1547), whose mixture of devout piety and Renaissance idealism was at the heart of the Italian movement that has been called "Catholic evangelism."[8]

Reginald Pole was eventually to absolve the kingdom from schism while he was only a deacon, which is an oddity in itself. He was to promulgate constitutions for the restoration of Catholicity in 1556, while still a deacon. Finally named archbishop of Canterbury, he would become a priest on March 20, 1556, and a bishop two days later, on March 22. On this occasion Paul IV promoted him to the rank of cardinal-priest. Out of legal scruple Pole had not wished to be made archbishop as long as Thomas Cranmer was alive, even when the see of Canterbury was made vacant by the excommunication of the archbishop. For Cranmer had been the lawful archbishop in the last year of Henry VIII. Cranmer was burnt for heresy on March 21, between Pole's ordination to the priesthood and his consecration to the episcopate, thus throwing a shadow on Reginald Pole's promotion. But this was apparently not a major consideration in the mind of anyone.

This digression on the life of Reginald Pole highlights the choice made by Julius III in 1553. Pole belonged to the reforming party in the Church, and he was a moderate. Although only a deacon, he was the most qualified of the English clergy to bring an end to the schism, and to reconcile the kingdom with the Holy See and the Catholic Church.

The Problem of the Married Clergy

In regard to the clergy, the chief practical problem related to the marriage of deacons, priests, and bishops. What should be done with the clergy that had entered marriage? Regarding the marriage of clergy, the civil law had been formulated in a royal proclamation of Henry VIII, of November 16, 1521, when, in the wake of the continental Reformation, reforming ideas were beginning to spread: married clergy were liable to deprivation of benefices and to imprisonment. But under Edward VI, the marriage of clergy, voted by the Commons in 1547, but rejected by the Lords, had been authorized by royal statute in February 1549.

Two facts had to be taken into account. On the one hand, many of the previously celibate clergy had married under Edward VI. The exact number is not known. But one can estimate that approximately one third of the diocesan clergy had married.[9] Among the religious, who had been forcibly secularized by the destruction of the monasteries, it is more hazardous to guess at the proportion of those who married. That there were a number of them, however, is certain, as they are mentioned in documents of the time of Queen Mary. On the other hand, there had been relatively few ordinations in the last years of Henry VIII and under Edward VI. As one may well realize in the aftermath of Vatican Council II, periods of spiritual turmoil are not conducive to many lasting vocations to the priesthood or the religious life! Given the high number of married clergy and the small number of recent ordinations, deprivation, degradation to the lay state, or imprisonment could only be measures of last resort. The concern of Queen Mary's government and of her bishops was that as many as possible of the priests who had incurred canonical irregularities be restored to their ministry, after separation from their wives (in the case of the secular clergy) or divorce (imposed on the religious), and a suitable penitence.

Action had to be taken. The queen could not wait for the legate's arrival in England. Cardinal Pole was delayed by several circumstances. He visited emperor Charles V, the queen's great uncle, and the king of France, Francis I, in order to gain their support for his mission and to urge them not to engage in war against each other. In addition, the emperor managed by sundry means to postpone the legate's departure for England. He preferred the matter of religion to be settled directly by the queen, with the advice of his own ambassador. And he wanted no interference in the delicate matter of the queen's marriage. Meanwhile, Mary herself was indeed eager that the pope should approve and bless the Catholic restoration that she was initiating by virtue of the royal supremacy. Yet it was unlikely that parliament could be persuaded to do this, unless it was certain that those who had profited from the alienation of church properties and the spoliation of the monasteries under Henry VIII would not be forced to give anything back to the Church. The pope's agreement to the non-restitution of church goods had to be obtained first.

Due to this combination of causes, the legate was unable to enter England before November 1554. By that time, the queen had deposed most of the bishops who had been appointed by Edward VI. Several official reasons had been given for the deprivations: attempted marriage and refusal to repudiate their wife; denial of papal authority and heresy; only in the case of John Taylor (c.1503-1554), Edwardine bishop of Lincoln since 1552, was the reason clearly given as "nullity of consecration."[10] The queen had also quelled several uprisings provoked by the unpopularity of her matrimonial projects, and she had effectively married her Spanish cousin, the emperor's son, the future Philip II. The marriage was celebrated in Winchester cathedral on July 25, 1554.

In the meantime, with the help of the Catholic bishops who in retirement, in jail, or in exile had survived the reign of Edward VI, the queen tried to advance the cause of true religion. A Catholic clergy had to be provided for the people. The proceedings that were followed before Pole's arrival are abundantly illustrated from the archives of British dioceses. The bishops of Queen Mary depose clergy for reason of *haeresis bigamiae,* the "heresy of bigamy:"[11] married to the Church by virtue of their orders, priests have, in addition, married a woman whom they now refuse to leave. The bishops reconcile with the Catholic Church, and restore to their ministry, though not in their previous location, married clergy who have repudiated their wife and repented. They also depose false clergy, laymen who somehow have invaded a parish and functioned as priests (there were a few).[12] But they do not commonly depose a deacon, priest, or bishop for the sole reason of their having been ordained according to the Ordinals of 1550 or 1552.

The principles are clearly expounded in a series of eighteen articles that were sent by the queen to the bishop of London, Edmund Bonner (c.1500-1569, bishop in 1540), on March 4, 1554:

—(n. 1) The canons and laws to be enforced are those "heretofore in the time of King Henry VIII used within this realm of England and the dominions of the same, not being direct and expressly contrary to the laws and statutes of this realm."[13]

—(n. 2) The bishops must be careful "that no person be admitted or received to any ecclesiastical function, benefit, or office, being a sacramentary infected or defamed with any notable kind of heresy or other great crime." More simply, no heretic is to be ordained, or, if previously ordained, allowed to function in an ecclesiastical office. ("Sacramentary" designates someone who professes Zwingli's doctrines in regard to the sacraments).

—(n. 7) All who "contrary to the state of their order and the laudable custom of the Church, have married and used women as their wives, or otherwise notably and slanderously disordered and abused themselves" must be deprived. (f. 90)

—(n. 8) Those, however, who have been widowed or who "with the consents of their wives or women openly in the presence of the bishop do profess to abstain" may be given ecclesiastical functions again, though not in the same location.

—(n. 9) The religious, "having solemnly professed chastity," who have fallen into the same disorder must "be divorced every one from his said woman."

Dudum cum charissima

Detailed instructions had been promised in *Post nuntium nobis.* They were not sent until much later, after Pole, who could gauge the depth of the problems facing the Church from his constant correspondence with the queen and with the English bishops, had requested them.

Dudum cum charissima, of March 8, 1554, begins with a general description of Pole's mission. The legate is "fully to absolve and to free in both forums—the [internal] forum of conscience and the [external] forum of the courts—and to unite with the community of the other faithful . . ."[14] all those, "of both sexes, laity as well as secular clergy, and regulars of all orders, even those in sacred orders, and of whatever state, degree, condition and quality," whether they have episcopal, archiepiscopal, or patriarchal dignity, or the worldly dignity of marquis, duke, or king . . . [who are] "the followers of whatever heresies or new sects," even if they have relapsed," provided that they acknowledge their error, repent them, and humbly ask to be received in the orthodox faith . . . " There is no limit to the legate's power of absolution. He may absolve all persons from "sins (heresies, apostasies, blasphemies, and whatever other errors . . .), crimes, excesses, delicts," including the penalties of "excommunication, suspension, interdict, and other ecclesiastical and temporal corporal punishments, capital sentences, censures, and pains," even if such persons have lain under these penalties for more than twenty years, and even when the absolution of their sins is canonically reserved to the pope and the apostolic see.

Turning to specific problems of the clergy, Paul IV envisages several cases, in which the legate has also full power of absolution. He may absolve, (1) those who have "celebrated masses and other divine offices against (*contra*) the rites and ceremonies hitherto approved and customary, or have mixed other ceremonies with them," (2) those who have been guilty of "bigamy." In the context, bigamy means that, being already married to the Church by ordination, they have also married, or attempted to marry, a woman.

In regard to the value of the orders of such persons, the bull distinguishes four cases.

—Firstly, some were "properly and lawfully ordained before falling into this heresy."[15] The heresy in question is that of bigamy, the marriage of priests. For this is the only specific heresy that has been previously mentioned. That the expression would designate the "Anglican heresy in general" is a misreading. "Properly and lawfully" (*rite ac legitime*) I understand to refer to the liceity of ordination, which of course implies its validity.

—Secondly, there are those who have never been "promoted to an order by their ordinary."[16] A few such usurpations of ecclesiastical functions are known to have taken place under Edward VI. The legate may promote those persons to orders if they are otherwise suitable, provided that they have been absolved in the sacrament of penance. He may even wave the obligation of making a public abjuration. There is no chance that the expression could designate the clergy ordained according to the Ordinal. This is in fact the next category.

—Thirdly, another case is envisagd after discussion of several incidental problems: the non-observance of Lent and of the laws of fast and abstinence, the marriage of secular clergy with "virgins [that is, nuns] or with corrupt secular women,"[17] the possession of various ecclesiastical benefices, and the power of the legate to share his authority with others by delegation and subdelegation. This third case relates to

> orders that they never or badly (*nunquam aut male*) received, and to the episcopal function that was conveyed to them by other heretical or schismatic bishops or archbishops, or otherwise less properly (*minus rite*) and the usual form of the Church not being followed.[18]

In this case also, the legate, who is still in Flanders, may "freely use" his full authority, even through delegates. There are two ambiguities in the text. First, it puts together some who "never" received orders and others who received them "badly." I take it, however, that *nunquam* cannot be identical with *male,* for the connecting word between them, *aut,* has the meaning of choice and distinction, unlike *seu* or *sive,* that would indicate identity and synonymity. Second, the text associates orders in general (*ordines*) and episcopal consecration (*munus consecrationis*), both having been received *minus rite.* I take it that *minus rite* means "illicitly," the illiceity being due to the use of another than "the customary form of the Church." Episcopacy and orders (the episcopate not being an order in the strict sense in the theology of the period, inherited from the Middle Ages)[19] are seen together from a liturgical point of view. Episcopacy is mentioned next, but it is then seen from a different angle.

—Fourthly, the last case is that of those bishops or archbishops who received their "metropolitan or other cathedral church from schismatic laity, especially from Henry and Edward, and intervened in their government and administration, and like true archbishops and bishops audaciously and in fact (*de facto*) [were] usurping their fruits, incomes, and benefices even for a very long time." Whether they fell into heresy after ordination, or were heretics before, the legate may reconcile them to the Church and rehabilitate them. He may even, if the queen so wishes, place them as bishops or archbishops in the same churches that they administered during the schism. It was in fact this fourth case that occasioned the bull *Dudum cum charissima.* By the beginning of 1554, the queen wanted to appoint five Henrician bishops to some of the sees that were left vacant by the deprivation of seven Edwardine bishops, who by then were either in exile or in jail. Her choice had to be confirmed by the legate. Reginald Pole, who was still lingering on the continent, had asked for further instructions from Rome.

The bull itself does not refer by name to the Ordinals of Edward VI. Yet the third case raises the question of ordination directly. One should identify the clergy of the first category (*rite et legitime*) as having been ordained with the old Ordinal, and the second (*nunquam*) as not having been ordained at all, even though they had acted as though ordained. The third category (*minus rite, male*) corresponds to those who had been effectively but not licitly ordained or consecrated: this is the clergy of the Edwardine Ordinals. The fourth category is that of bishops promoted in schism. Since the matter of when and how they were consecrated is not pursued here, one may assume that Cardinal Pole had the power to confirm them in the episcopate, whether they were consecrated with the old Pontifical or with the new Ordinals. As a matter of fact, however, none of this last group was reappointed by the queen.

Conclusion

Julius III entrusted Pole with absolute authority to settle all the problems that could arise in the reconciliation of the English Church and its clergy with the Catholic Church and the Holy See. It is equally clear that the pope gave his legate no detailed instructions regarding the ordinations that had taken place under Edward VI.

Such a complete confidence in Reginal Pole on the part of Pope Julius III may seem surprising to us. But it was genuine.

In fact, it was not confined to the problems of England. These extensive powers were exactly parallel to the instructions that the same pope gave his legate in the diplomatic field, in regard to the urgency of keeping the peace between Francis I and Charles V. The rivalry of these two Catholic sovereigns and their nations was seen by the pope as a danger for the whole Church. The support and cooperation of both were needed to settle the English matter. In the bull *Cum proximis superioribus,* of September 20, 1554, Julius III sent Cardinal Pole on a peace mission:

> We prescribe nothing to your prudence. But we grant [you] full and free authority and faculty to do, to discuss, to promise, in our name [and] for that purpose, all that you will judge to be compatible with our dignity and that of this Holy See.[20]

It is in the light of these broad legatine powers that one should read the queen's article 15 in the instructions that she gave the bishop of London in 1554:

> Concerning such persons as were heretofore promoted to any orders after the new sort and fashion of orders, considering they were not ordered in very deed, the bishop of the diocese, finding otherwise sufficiency and ability in these men, may supply that thing which wanted in them before, and then, according to his discretion, admit them to minister.[21]

The bishop, being subdelegated by the legate, is to supply, ceremonially or by decree, to whatever was missing in the "deed" of ordination done "after the new sort and fashion of orders." Neither is the queen talking about sacramental hylomorphism (the "matter and form" of a sacrament), nor is she asserting that such persons are not priests. She is only saying that there was a defect in their ordination, and that the defect should be remedied.

Chapter 3

Paul IV

Julius III died on March 21, 1555. Cardinal Carafa—Paul IV—was elected bishop of Rome on May 23, 1555, after a brief tenure of less than one month (April 9 to May 1) by Marcellus II. Like Pole and Contarini, Carafa had belonged to the reformist party among the cardinals. He had been one of the architects of the *Consilium de emendanda ecclesia.* But he was not a moderate; he was definitely an extremist. His wish that Cranmer be burnt for heresy is a token of this. Another may be seen in his customary designation of Henry VIII and Edward VI as "pretended kings," as though they had usurped the throne or other kings were available!

Queen Mary died on November 17, 1558, and Reginald Pole a few hours later on the same day. Elizabeth succeeded her sister, being immediately proclaimed queen by the conservative archbishop of York, Nicholas Heath. As early as Christmas day of 1558, when Elizabeth walked out of the royal chapel because the celebrant, acting against her orders, elevated the host at the consecration, her religious policy was clear. It became official when, in January 1559, her first parliament restored the royal supremacy. Paul IV had therefore time, before he died on August 18, 1559, to see the collapse of the work of his predecessor, of Queen Mary, and of Reginald Pole.

Two documents of Paul IV's pontificate are immediately relevant to the question of Anglican orders, *Praeclara charissimi,* of June 20, 1555, and *Regimini universalis ecclesiae,*

of October 30 of the same year, to which one ought to add
Dudum ecclesiae eboracensis.

Praeclara charissimi

This bull is addressed to Philip and Mary, "king and queen"
of England. It was issued by Pope Paul IV after they had sent
to Rome a delegation of three members, headed by the bishop
of Norwich, Thomas Thirlby (d. 1570). The purpose of this
mission was to explain the complexities of the English situation
to the new pope, and to obtain from him both a confirmation
of the policies of Julius III and a formal endorsement of the
measures adopted by the papal legate. Thirlby himself was a
former schismatic. He had been consecrated under Edward
VI, in April 1550, before the new Ordinal was adopted. He
had voted against the Ordinal in the House of Lords. He had
nevertheless accepted Edward's settlement, and he had even
used the Ordinal of 1552, at least for the ordination of a
deacon. He had been reconciled with the Church of Rome on
August 19, 1554, before Pole's arrival in England, and he was
in process of being transferred by the queen to Ely. In the
diplomatic language of *Praeclara charissimi,* however, he and
the other two members of his team were "endowed with every
virtue."[1]

As listed in the bull, the main problems that still need attention concern the following cases:

(1) marriages contracted in spite of canonical impediments
and the legitimacy of the offspring of such marriages;

(2) the status of sundry foundations that were made without
proper canonical authority;

(3) the present ownership of lands and other properties that
used to belong to the Church, and that cannot be returned
without causing enormous turmoil and disturbing the peace;

(4) the sentences of ecclesiastical tribunals that had no proper
jurisdiction;

(5) the status of the clergy.

In all these matters the pope approves in general whatever
the legate has done. Regarding matrimony, Paul IV specifies
that the laity who have contracted illicit marriage, "whether

with due knowledge or in ignorance" of impediments (*scienter vel ignoranter*), may "remain in these marriages freely and licitly, or contract them anew."[2] The formulation suggests that both ways are equivalent. The people may simply, with the legate's dispensation from the impediment, continue in their marriage; or, if they wish, they may, still with the proper dispensation, renew the ceremony of marriage.

Regarding the clergy, the bull addresses two different questions. Firstly, there is the situation of those who have obtained indults "concerning orders as well as ecclesiastical benefices or other spiritual matters" by virtue of the "pretended authority of the Supremacy of the Church of England." Such indults were obtained invalidly (*nulliter*) and *de facto* (that is, not *de jure,* not according to the law). The pope endorses the legate's decisions to grant the necessary dispensations so "that they may remain in their orders and benefices."[3] The question of the validity of orders is raised. The indults had no value, but, whether or not one can make the logical inference that the orders thus received were also null, the legate has granted the necessary dispensations to continue in such orders. The pope approves these measures.

Secondly, the bull faces the question of recognizing orders received during the schism. Pope Paul puts down a condition for accepting them. That this is important is manifest: the condition appears twice, in slightly different wording:

> In such a way that, if some were promoted to sacred or non-sacred order by another than a bishop or archbishop who had been licitly and properly ordained, they are bound to receive these orders again from their ordinary, and must not exercise ministry in the meantime.[4]

In other words, all orders given during the schism are accepted, whatever the rite used, as long as the ordaining bishop had himself been ordained *rite et recte,* that is, according to the old Pontifical. The ministrations of the bishops who were ordained with the Ordinals of 1550 and 1552 are not accepted. It is clear that the urgent question is no longer that of married priests and deacons. Presumably, most of these cases have been taken care of. Paul IV's main concern is now to make sure that nothing may be interpreted as an approval of actions performed by virtue of the royal supremacy, for such actions were schismatic in intention and in reality. There were two sorts of bishops at the end of King Edward's reign. The newer ones had been promoted to the episcopate with the Ordinal. The older ones had been consecrated with the Sarum Pontifical. All were schismatic, advanced during the schism. Several of Henry's bishops who kept their see under Edward VI had even shared the heresies of the king and his archbishop, Cranmer. All of them could be presumed to have used the Ordinal for the promotion of ordinands when the Ordinal had become legal to the exclusion of all previous rites.

This being the case, the bishops who are designated in the bull as *rite et recte ordinati* can only be those who were consecrated under the old rite, before the Ordinals of 1550 and 1552. But the status of the new Edwardine bishops in relation to the sacrament of orders is not explained at this point. The most logical way to understand the pope's decision is to see it as disciplinary rather than dogmatic. The pope wants the acts of Edward VI's bishops to be ignored, treated as non-existent. Yet he does not raise the precise question of the sacramental forms of the Ordinal, or whether the episcopal charism had in fact been imparted to these bishops.

Dudum ecclesiae eboracensis

Someone in the Vatican offices made an astonishing mistake in 1555, when Mary Tudor wished to transfer and promote Nicholas Heath (d. 1579), bishop of Worcester, to York. The bull from the Holy See instructed Heath to receive episcopal consecration from a bishop, assisted by two or three others, all of them "having the grace and communion of the Apostolic See."[5] Heath, however, was a bishop since 1540. He had been consecrated with the Pontifical. In the terms of *Praeclara charissimi,* he was *rite et recte ordinatus.* The consternation caused by the papal bull forced Reginald Pole to ask for clarification. This came in two forms. Another bull was addressed to Nicholas Heath: *Dudum ecclesiae eboracensis,* and a more inclusive brief was sent to Pole, *Regimini universalis ecclesiae.* The two documents bear the same date, October 30, 1555.

Dudum ecclesiae eboracensis tries to explain the mistake. It reviews the facts. Heath had received his orders from schismatic bishops, who had been "ordained and consecrated in the form of the Church, and therefore who were lacking only the fulness of the episcopal order."[6] He had himself been "marked with the clerical character according to the same form."[7] He had been made bishop of Rochester and then of Worcester "by the pretended king Henry or Edward," and consecrated by at least three schismatic bishops "who had been ordained and consecrated with the same form, and who therefore were lacking only the fulness of the episcopal order." But none of this had been mentioned in the document previously received in Rome about Heath's transfer to York. Hence the mistake! Even now, however, *Dudum ecclesiae eboracensis* shows that Rome is still not well informed. It is not quite sure whether Heath was made a bishop under Henry or under Edward. Furthermore, Rome is under the impression that Heath had functioned as unconsecrated bishop of Rochester and of Worcester before finally being consecrated! In fact, Heath was elected to Rochester in 1539, consecrated in April 1540, and transferred to Worcester in 1543, all this under Henry!

The significant point of this document is that the schismatic bishops consecrated according to the old Pontifical are said to be "lacking only the fulness of the episcopal order." At least I cannot find a better translation of the Latin expression, *executione ordinis episcopalis carentibus.* As I understand it, this relates to the fact that their election was not confirmed by the bishop of Rome. The fulness in question is not sacramental. It is the fulness of authority or jurisdiction that comes from endorsement or sponsorship by the bishop of Rome as primate in the universal Church and, as one would say after Vatican Council II, in the episcopal college. The acceptance of the royal supremacy during the ceremony of consecration was a sign that this fulness was lacking. The rite had been altered to fit the situation of the Henrician Church. Henry had replaced the oath of allegiance to the bishop of Rome by an oath of allegiance to himself as "supreme head of the Church of England" and by a promise of obedience to one's archbishop.

In the eyes of Paul IV this entailed a deficiency in what had been received. Yet this deficiency was not such as to impede reception of the episcopate as such.

Regimini universalis ecclesiae

This brief, addressed to Reginald Pole, is the second document composed to remedy the mishap in the matter of Heath's promotion to York. Its purpose is immediately stated: "that all ecclesiastical persons may minister with pure heart and healthy conscience in the orders that they have received."[8] The text states that Paul IV has recently approved the papal legate's proceedings in the case of "secular ecclesiastics and regular persons," who had obtained *nulliter et de facto,* from the "pretended authority of the Supremacy of the Church of England,". . . "diverse requests, dispensations, graces, and indults which concern [*concernentia*] orders as well as ecclesiastical benefices or other spiritual matters."[9]

This formula is borrowed from *Praeclara charissimi.* By using it again, the pope clearly shows that he is restating the policy already endorsed in the previous bull. He is thereby reaffirming the measures by which Reginald Pole "gave dispensation so that they could remain in their orders and benefices." Once again the condition is added: the ordaining bishops must have themselves been ordained with the Pontifical.[10] This proviso is repeated immediately in identical wording.

Paul IV then proceeds to clarify the point. There has been some hesitancy as to the identity of the bishops and archbishops who "during the schism of the kingdom could be said to be licitly and rightly ordained."[11] The pope wishes to lift this hesitancy and assure "the serenity of conscience of those who were promoted to orders during the said schism."[12] He therefore restates the principle more clearly (*clarius exprimendo*):

> Only those bishops and archbishops cannot be said to have been ordained licitly and rightly, who were not ordained and consecrated in the form of the Church; and therefore the persons whom they promoted to those orders did not receive the orders, but must receive them again from their

ordinary, in keeping with the content and tenor of our letters, and they are bound to it. The others—to whom these orders were given by bishops and archbishops who had been ordained and consecrated in the form of the Church, even though those bishops and archbishops were schismatics and received the churches over which they presided from Henry VIII and Edward VI, pretended kings of England,—did receive the character of the orders given to them, and were only lacking in regard to the fulness of the same orders . . .[13]

Undoubtedly, it seems inconsistent to the modern Catholic mind to admit implicitly the ordination of deacons and priests through the Ordinal, while explicitly rejecting the sacramental actions performed by bishops consecrated according to the same Ordinal. But this was by no means illogical in the theological context of the sixteenth century. This may be illustrated with three considerations.

The first touches the nature of episcopacy. In the sixteenth century, as in scholasticism and in the canonical organization of the medieval Church, episcopacy, even if it was often called an order, was not universally considered to be a sacrament. Only with Vatican Council II was episcopacy solemnly declared to be sacramental in the full sense of the term. In the sixteenth century as in the Middle Ages, it could very well be maintained that episcopacy was the highest degree of the sacrament of orders, not by virtue of a sacramental grace or a "character" received in consecration, but by virtue of a jurisdiction received from the bishop of Rome, successor and vicar of Peter. This in fact had been St. Thomas Aquinas's understanding of the matter. The sacrament of order, Aquinas had written, includes the seven degrees of porter, lector, exorcist, acolyte, subdeacon, deacon, and priest.[14] Episcopacy is not in the list. It is not counted as a distinct order. For, in the strict sacramental sense, a sacerdotal order is tied to the eucharist,[15] and a bishop "has no power superior to a priest in this regard."[16] In a secondary and non-sacramental sense, an order may be defined as "an office regarding some sacred actions." In this sense, episcopacy is an order, since a bishop "has power above a priest in the hierarchic actions that regard the mystical body." Episcopacy is a "power (*potestas*) given along with some sort of consecration (*cum quadam consecratione*)."[17] No "character" is conveyed in the promotion of a bishop, "since by it a man is not related directly to God, but to the mystical body of Christ."[18] St. Thomas is also of the opinion that heretical bishops "confer true sacraments, but do not give grace through them, not because of sacramental inefficacy, but on account of the sins of those who receive sacraments from them against the Church's prohibition."[19]

The judgment of Pope Paul IV on the Edwardine bishops followed this scholastic approach to the sacrament of orders. Theologically, the bishops of the Ordinal were not given any *potestas* over the mystical body of Christ, because, canonically, they received no jurisdiction from the bishop of Rome. Their acts were therefore illegitimate. But in this matter it was not the Ordinal as such that was at fault. It was the schism of the royal supremacy, compounded by heresy under Edward VI. In order to fix a clear standard of discrimination between what was acceptable and what was not, Paul IV drew the line at the historical point when the new Ordinal was imposed by Edward VI, in 1550.

Admittedly, the pope and his legate could have drawn the line differently. They could have chosen the accession of Edward VI as the point of no return to orthodoxy. They could have drawn a merely temporal line, deciding on a date after which the English ordinations to the episcopate were not acceptable. They preferred another method. The line they drew was liturgical: ordination through the Ordinal imposed on the Church of England by the royal supremacy indicated that the bishops thus ordained had no jurisdiction. Having no jurisdiction, they had no episcopal power and authority. Having neither jurisdiction nor power, they could not effectively ordain anyone. But the pope's decision said nothing about the liturgy of the Ordinal. Again, it was not the ritual as such that was the problem. It was the exclusion of the papal primacy. The pope's line of thought rested on the premise that liturgical ordination to the episcopate is not sacramental in the strict sense: it does little more than solemnize the granting of episcopal jurisdiction by the bishop of Rome. Or, since most bishops were then elected by a canonical chapter after a congé d'élire had been received from the king or queen, ordination signifies the canonical confirmation of their election. Whatever the liturgical tenor of the Ordinal, it could not be considered the proper means for making a bishop, because neither king nor queen has any power to grant episcopal jurisdiction.

"Form and matter"

The second consideration has to do with the state of the question, in the sixteenth century, concerning the "form and matter" of the sacrament of orders. In this context, the use of the word, "form," has its origin in the theory of Aristotle on "hylomorphism." Form is a correlate of matter, matter and form being defined as principles whose conjunction makes a creaturely being what it is. The theological application of this notion to sacraments is analogical: two aspects of a sacrament are compared to the matter and the form of a being. As generally identified in scholastic theology, the material elements (bread, wine, oil, gestures) of a sacrament were seen as its matter, the spiritual elements (prayers, words, expressions of intent) as its form. It follows that intention and form go together: where the form that is used by the minister is recognized by the faithful as customary in the Church, the Church's intent is properly assumed to be present.

In the supplement of the *Summa,* Thomas Aquinas held that, since "this sacrament principally consists in a power received," the form of the sacrament of orders must express power, which is done by the use of the imperative.[20] Thomas does not, at this point, look at the sense of the words that constitute the form. But the fact is that the scholastics were not quite sure what the form of ordination was. In Supp., q. 34, a. 5, ad 3, Thomas argued that both the porrection of the instruments by the bishop (a medieval rite of Gallican origin) and the touching of them by the candidate, pertain to "the sense of the sacrament." If such is the case, then they are the matter of the sacrament, the form being the words that accompany them: "*Accipe potestatem offerendi sacrificium in ecclesia pro vivis et mortuis, in nomine Patris et Filii et Spiritus Sancti.*" However, sacramental hylomorphism, though generally accepted among the scholastics, was not understood in the same way by all theologians. St. Bonaventure stayed nearer to the non-Aristotelian language of St. Augustine. Unlike St. Thomas, he never asked what was the matter and what the form of a sacrament; he preferred to speak of sign (*sensibile signum*) and signification (*spirituale sive sacrum signatum*).[21]

Furthermore, since the consecration of a bishop was not understood sacramentally, there could be no question of matter and form in the usual sense. In the traditional rites of the Pontifical there was indeed a kind of porrection of the instruments, when the Bible was placed over the head of the bishop-elect, and when the symbolic instrument of pastoral leadership, the crozier, was put in his hand. One could, by analogy, find in it form and matter: the laying on of hands, or the placing of the Bible, or the handing on of the crozier, could be the matter, while the accompanying words said by the consecrating bishop would be the form.

At the Council of Florence, the decree for the Armenians (November 22, 1439) specified the matter and form of the sacrament of orders, though on the descriptive rather than the prescriptive mode: these are the porrection of the instruments with the accompanying formula, "*Accipe . . .*"[22] But since episcopacy was not seen as a sacrament, the decree said nothing about its matter and form. As a point of fact, Reginald Pole generally followed the decree for the Armenians. On February 4, 1556, he issued a series of instructions or decrees on Catholic reform, that embody his understanding of his mission. The second decree explains the seven sacraments of the Catholic tradition. When he comes to the sacrament of orders, Pole writes:

> The sixth sacrament is that of orders. Its matter is that through transmission of which the order is given. The presbyterate is given through porrection of the chalice with wine and the paten with bread; the diaconate through giving the book of the gospels; the subdiaconate through tradition of an empty chalice surmounted by an empty paten; and likewise the other [minor] orders through the things that pertain to their ministry. The form of the priesthood is this: "Receive the power to offer sacrifice in the Church for the

living and the dead, in the name of the Father, the Son, and the Holy Spirit . . ."[23]

This endorsement of the decree for the Armenians had in fact no other effect than explaining the porrection of the instruments in the Pontifical. It had no consequence on acceptance or refusal of the ceremonies of the Ordinal.

"Form and Manner"

The third consideration touches on the use of the term, "form," in the documents of Paul IV. There was another usage of the word in legal and canonical literature that owed nothing to Aristotle. Paul IV's view of the orders given in the schismatic Church of England could not ignore the legal measures that had been adopted by king and parliament concerning the making of bishops. When Henry VIII outlawed the authority of the see of Rome and its bishop in his own dominions, he referred to "every person and persons being hereafter chosen, elected, nominated, presented, invested, and consecrated to the dignity or office of any Archbishop or Bishop within this realm, or within any other the King's dominions, according to the *form,* tenor, and effect of this present act . . ."[24] This is not a hylomorphic use of the word, form. The term designates the general and specific regulations of the Act, that henceforth have force of law. Likewise, Edward VI's *Act to order the drawing up of a new form of ordination,* of 1549, spoke of "such form and manner of making and consecrating Archbishops, Bishops, Priests, Deacons, and other Ministers of the Church . . ." That "form and manner" are not meant in the Aristotelian sense is made evident by the fact that there have never been any sacramental "form and matter" connected with the making of an archbishop. In terms of ordination, an archbishop is no more than a bishop. It follows that the "form and manner of making and consecrating Archbishops, Bishops, Priests and Deacons," that constitute the Ordinal annexed to the Book of Common Prayer of 1552, is not the form of the sacrament of orders. It is the whole Ordinal, the general ordering of the liturgy of ordination and consecration.

Paul IV's use of the term, form, in *Regimini universalis ecclesiae* is identical. The persons who were not "ordained and consecrated *in forma ecclesiae*" are precisely those who were subjected to the new "form and manner of making and consecrating . . . etc . . ." of Edward VI. Nothing is stated or implied concerning the theological question of the "form and matter" of the sacrament of orders.

Paul IV's Central Concern

Given the sacramental theology inherited from the Middle Ages, the reasoning of Paul IV is entirely consistent. Neither the pope nor his legate is primarily interested in the matter and form of the sacrament of orders. In the fashion of the decree to the Armenians, the specific matter and form of the Pontifical do not belong in the dogmatic area; they pertain to the catechetical, liturgical, and pastoral order. Paul IV is concerned about the "fashion and manner" of making priests and bishops. Used by a bishop with the proper jurisdiction, as signified by his consecration after the "fashion and manner" of the Church, even when this bishop was schismatic under Henry VIII or Edward VI, the "form and manner" of making a priest according to the Ordinal could truly make a priest.

Yet the episcopate is not, like the priesthood, an order. It does not come under the same rules. The "form and manner" of making a bishop in the Ordinal did not make a bishop, because this form and manner excluded the authority of the bishop of Rome that was necessarily involved in making a bishop. At the hands of such Edwardian bishops, neither the form and manner of the Ordinal made a priest, nor would those of the Pontifical have made one, had any of those bishops, per chance, used the old rite.

The difference between the two popes is now clear. At the time of Julius III the papal legate is given full authority to reconcile with the Holy See and the Catholic Church all who wish for reconciliation. The page may be turned over their schism and even heresy, if now they profess true Catholic doctrine. Married deacons, priests, and bishops, however, must repudiate their wife and return to the discipline of celibacy if they wish to function in the clergy. At the time of Paul IV, those who so wished have been reconciled. The old discipline has been restored. Yet, Cranmer remaining adamant in his heresies, the see of Canterbury becomes vacant. At the hands of Mary Tudor, the royal supremacy favors the Catholics, but, as intended by Henry VIII and Edward VI, and as interpreted by Cranmer, it denies, and takes the place of, the Roman primacy. It is now important to make sure that none of the works of Cranmer will remain. The leniency of the legate and the pope toward those who have previously faulted must not be seen as somehow countenancing the works of the felon archbishop. The way to destroy his works, before destroying his person by fire, is opened by the traditional distinction between priest and bishop. A rite that pretends to make a bishop against the Roman primacy suffers from the inner contradiction of denying a power that is, in the West, at the time, considered essential to the making of a bishop. The orders thus given, and the episcopate thus transmitted, are defective; they lack a certain fulness, the fulness that comes from being endorsed by the Roman Pontiff. In the case of Heath, the fulness is lacking by rejection of the Roman primacy; yet Heath is truly a bishop. In the case of one who would be consecrated according to the Ordinal, the two successive affirmations of the royal supremacy have a cumulative effect that makes the defect more damaging.

When Paul IV enquires about the rite that has been used to make a bishop, he does not ask if the matter and form of the Ordinal are capable of conveying the sacrament of orders and its higher degree, episcopacy. He is not giving an answer to the modern question of validity, for this is not his question. The modern question, that was already that of Leo XIII, takes for granted that the ordainer is acting as a bishop, and places the whole burden of transmitting orders on the matter and form used by this bishop. The picture is different for Paul IV. Form and matter are irrelevant. What is relevant is that some bishops, because they denied the papal primacy at their ordination, have functioned as false bishops. The testimony against them is the Ordinal in which they were ordained. But Paul IV's way of drawing a line of no return says nothing about the capacity of the Ordinal as such, if and when in the proper hands, to convey the sacrament of orders. In the meantime, however, the pope had planted a time bomb in the fabric of the Church of England. He had not condemned the Ordinal as such. But the time would soon come when no one could properly use it, for no one would be left who had been made a bishop according to the Pontifical.

Conclusion

When Paul IV tried to clarify these questions, the queen hoped for an heir to continue her work. Somewhat later, this hope was frustrated. Still later, six years after coming to power, Mary Tudor fell sick and died, to be succeeded by the moderately Protestant Elizabeth. Paul IV died in the first year of Elizabeth's reign. The task of dealing with the new situation in England was then left to Pius IV (pope on December 25, 1555, d. 1565), who just waited for things to happen, and to Pius V (elected on January 7, 1566, d. 1572), who drew his own conclusion and excommunicated Elizabeth, "the pretended queen."

Chapter 4

Pius V

The historical investigation of the matter of Anglican orders should take cognizance of the judgment of the Catholic Recusants, under Queen Elizabeth, regarding the value of the Ordinal. The Recusants were those who rejected Elizabeth's version of the royal supremacy, because they continued to profess the supremacy or primacy of the bishop of Rome over all other bishops in the Church. Many went into exile on the Continent, chiefly in French or Spanish territories, more rarely in Italy or at Rome itself. Some remained hidden or at least silent in England. A number of those who fled volunteered later for the "English mission." They were chiefly Jesuits and secular priests trained in English seminaries abroad. They formed the hard core of the continuing Catholicism of the British Isles, and many gave their life for their faith when, in 1570, Queen Elizabeth abandoned the relative leniency of her first years. Elizabeth's anger was of course due to Pius V's excommunication of herself, and above all to the pope's arrogant contention that her subjects were no longer bound by her laws. By the terms of the excommunication, the Recusants were rebels. Henceforth, she actively pressured and persecuted the followers of the bishop of Rome.

The Consecration of Matthew Parker

Elizabeth succeeded her sister Mary on November 17, 1558. She entered London on November 23. As early as December

9, the new chancellor, Nicholas Bacon, invited Matthew Parker to come to the capital in order to be made archbishop of Canterbury. Parker (1504-1575) had been ordained a priest in 1527 while studying at Cambridge.[1] He had married in 1547. He was Master of Corpus Christi College in Cambridge and dean of Lincoln at Mary's accession. Under Mary he had not abandoned his wife. Dispossessed of his benefices, he had led a quiet and studious life in a friend's house until the queen's death. Elizabeth, who frowned on clerical marriage, never restored the act of Edward VI that authorized it. But she was enough of a realist to ignore the issue and to tolerate married priests and bishops. Parker was her choice for the see of Canterbury, that had been made vacant by Reginald Pole's death.

Although Parker was reluctant to accept, he consented on August 6, 1559, after being duly elected by the chapter of Canterbury. According to the statutes of Henry VIII, four bishops at least must take part in the consecration of an archbishop. The queen therefore sent letters patent to several bishops, giving them the responsibility of confirming Parker's election and of ordaining him to the episcopate.

The first letters patent were sent to three of Mary's bishops, who were still unimpeded in their sees (Anthony Kitchin [1477-1563] of Llandaf, a former Benedictine abbot, and a bishop since 1545, David Pole of Peterborough, Gilbert Bourne of Bath and Wells) and to two bishops who had been deposed under Mary (William Barlow and John Scory). Among them, only Scory had been consecrated with the Ordinal. At the end of May 1559, however, the queen appointed a commission to administer to all ecclesiastics an oath accepting the royal supremacy as included in the new Act of Uniformity. All the bishops of Mary, except Kitchin, refused the oath and were deposed.

New letters patent were then sent to Anthony Kitchin, William Barlow, former bishop of Bath, now elected to Chichester, John Scory, former bishop of Chichester, now of Hereford, Miles Coverdale, former bishop of Exeter, Richard (or, as he is called in the document, John) Hodgkin, suffragan of Bedford, John Salisbury, suffragan of Thetford, and John Bale, of Ossory. Three had been ordained, under King Henry, with the Pontifical. They were Kitchin, Barlow, and Hodgkin (a bishop since December 1537). The others were Edwardine bishops, ordained with the Ordinal. Evidently, Elizabeth wished to associate both sorts of bishops, of the Pontifical and of the Ordinal, in the consecration of Parker. In order to make sure that everything would be regular and proper, the second letters patent included a curious clause, *Supplentes,* by which the queen "supplied" by her supreme authority whatever might be defective in the proceedings. It was of course dubious whether, having no canonical value, this royal version of the adage, *Ecclesia supplet,* had any legal standing. But the clause was in the logic of the royal supremacy: the sovereign would now do what used to be reserved to the pope. The queen's new secretary of State, Cecil, who was a strict constructionist in regard to law, must have entertained his own doubts about the legality of the matter. For safety's sake, he obtained a formal approbation of the letters patent by six prominent lawyers.

Anthony Kitchin managed somehow not to take part in the proceedings. The others confirmed the election. In the morning of December 17, 1559, Parker was consecrated in the chapel of Lambeth palace, by Barlow, Scory, Coverdale, and Hodgkin. The ceremony followed the Ordinal of 1552. It is notable that in the preceding May, parliament, dominated by Puritans, had debated a bill to the effect that there should be no "rites and ceremonies" in the making of bishops: the feelings of the Puritans were ignored. But, one could ask, had the Ordinal been made legal by the Act of Uniformity, in which it was not mentioned? Secretary Cecil did not think so. Only in 1566 did parliament, in order to remove all doubt, pronounce that the Ordinal was part of the Book of Common Prayer as approved under the Act of Uniformity.

The consecration of Parker to the episcopate is described at length in the official record that is included in the registers of the Church of Canterbury.

The "Great Controversy"

It is in the polemical writings of the Recusants that Elizabeth's bishops are openly accused of being false bishops. Both before and after the fatal year of 1570, when Pius V excommunicated the queen and her supporters, the reign of Elizabeth was the theater of sharp theological polemics between Anglican and Catholic authors. The Recusants had ample opportunity in these exchanges to express doubt about Anglican ordinations, or to call their adversaries false priests or false bishops, appellations that would have been mild compared to the excessive language that was commonly applied to theological adversaries. In fact, many of them did so, although most of the polemics were not focused on this point. The Recusants' rejection of the Anglican episcopate started shortly before the pope's excommunication of the queen. One can even pinpoint the moment when Anglican orders began to be called null and void, or various equivalents of this expression in the polemical language of the times: this took place in a virulent exchange of writings that opposed Thomas Harding to John Jewel.

The context was provided by what has been called the "great controversy" of Elizabethan times. The controversy was occasioned by a sermon delivered at Paul's Cross, in the heart of London, by John Jewel (1522-1571), a Marian exile who had recently been made bishop of Salisbury. In his sermon of November 25, 1559, Jewel, somewhat rashly, challenged "any learned man of all our adversaries" to find "any one sufficient sentence, out of any old Catholic doctor or father; or out of any old general Council; or any one example of the primitive Church, whereby it may be clearly and plainly proved that there was any private mass in the whole world at that time, for the space of six hundred years after Christ . . ."[2] A number of additional points, most of them relating to the eucharist, were included in the same challenge. In a later version of the sermon, delivered also at Paul's Cross on March 31, 1560, Jewel extended his list of articles to twenty-seven. Further, he promised that if such authority was produced by anyone, he would himself be "content to yield unto him and to subscribe."[3]

Being thus challenged, the Catholics responded in kind. Jewel then answered some of them, arguing that they had not produced the necessary evidence in support of their doctrines. The controversy lasted to the end of Jewel's life. Over sixty books or pamphlets were printed.[4]

Harding versus Jewel

Thomas Harding (1516-1572) had himself been schismatic.

Like Jewel, he had been ordained under Edward VI before 1551, and, according to Jewel's testimony, by the same bishop.[5] The first Ordinal was in force at the time. Harding had functioned as chaplain to the marquis of Dorset, Lady Jane Grey's father. He had known and admired the Italian reformer Peter Martyr. Jewel and Harding had known each other at the University of Oxford. Both had wavered in their allegiances. Harding had returned to Rome at the accession of Queen Mary, never to change again. Under Henry, Jewel had subscribed to Catholic articles concerning the sacrament and the mass as a "sacrifice propitiatory."[6] He had rejected them under Edward, had again recanted under Mary, had later fled to Francfort, and, on his return to England under Elizabeth, he had publicly apologized and repented his temporary papism. Harding and Jewel had met on Jewel's return; and Harding was later able to ask Jewel: "Did you not tell me that it [the Supremacy of the temporal Princes over the Church of England] stood neither with Scripture, nor with the Doctors, nor with the judgment of the Learned men of Germany, Geneva, and the parts where you had been?"[7]

After the Paul's Cross sermon, Jewel wrote his *Apologia ecclesiae anglicanae* (1562). In rebuttal, Harding published *An Answer to Maister Jewel's Challenge* (1564), *A Confutation of a Book entitled An Apology of the Church of England* (1565), *A Detection of Sundry Foul Errors* (1568), and a few shorter pieces. Jewel's most bulky response is *A Defense of the Apology of the Church of England* (1567), that is directed against Harding's *Confutation*.

The debate between the two was personal no less than theological. As was then common in theological polemics, they insulted each other copiously, with all the more bitterness as they knew each other, and each could accuse the other of inconstancy in faith and doctrine. That Anglican bishops are not bishops at all is expressed bluntly by Harding:

> Whatsoever you mean by your minister and by that office, this are we assured of, that in this your new church bishops, priests, deacons, subdeacons, or any other inferior orders, ye have none.[8]

Indeed, Harding refuses Jewel the title of bishop. In *A Detection of Sundry Foul Errors,* of 1568, he writes: "Truly, touching your dignity, what account so ever you make of yourself, I take you but for M. Jewel, bachelor of divinity, some time person of Sunningwel between Oxford and Abington. And that is the greatest degree that ever I knew you called unto."[9] The queen has given him the benefice of the bishopric of Salisbury. But "it is not money that can set you one step higher in ecclesiastical degree. A bishop you are not, I am right sure, neither can all the Kings and Queens of the world, nor all the Parliaments of England, by their own only power and authority make you a lawful and true bishop."

Harding's denial of Jewel's orders was a polemical and a political statement. In what sense it was also theological and doctrinal is, however, the important question. Harding's theological reasons are briefly summed up in this sentence:

> . . . ye have abandoned the external sacrifice and priesthood of the New Testament, and have not in your sect consecrated bishops; and therefore, being without priests made with lawful laying on of hands, as Scripture requireth, all holy orders being given by bishops only, how can ye say that any among you can lawfully minister, or that ye have any lawful ministers at all?[10]

One may distinguish four ideas in this passage. *First,* the so-called Church of England has rejected the Catholic doctrine of the mass and of the priesthood. *Second,* Jewel does not stand in the succession of the former bishops of Salisbury, since he does not teach their doctrine. *Third,* since Jewel has his authority only from "letters patent of the prince," he was "not duly called"[11] and he stands in the position of the Donatists. As St. Augustine concluded, "*ergo,* your Zwinglian and Calvinist belief, Mr. Jewel, and of the rest of your fellows, is not catholic." *Fourth,* Jewel's vocation or calling is non-existent, since "he was not lawfully made a priest, nor with churchly laying on of hands consecrated." In addition, Harding proclaims that Jewel and others have thrown doubt on their own doctrine, for they have not disciplined those preachers who assert that "every man, yea, and every woman be a priest."[12]

Jewel's refutation of the fundamental point is forceful. He rejects the doctrine of transubstantiation. He also denies that Christ can now be offered up "unto God his Father," for this was done once for all by himself. Yet he firmly believes that the eucharist is a sacrifice. This, however, should be properly understood. In keeping with Article XXXI, there is no room for "sacrifices of masses" offered for the dead. Yet, the bishop of Sarum maintains,

> we have the sacrifice of prayer, the sacrifice of alms-deeds, the sacrifice of praise, the sacrifice of thanksgiving, and the sacrifice of the death of Christ. We are taught to present our bodies as a pure and holy and pleasing sacrifice unto God, and to offer up unto him the burning oblation of our lips . . . Howbeit, if we speak of a sacrifice propitiatory for the satisfaction of sins, we have no other but only Christ Jesus the Son of God upon his cross . . . God's name be blessed for ever! We want neither church nor priesthood, nor any kind of sacrifice that Christ hath left unto his faithful.[13]

Taken together, the "sacrifice of thanksgiving" and the "sacrifice of the death of Christ" may be taken to express the Catholic eucharistic tradition. The note on the "sacrifice propitiatory" is entirely compatible with the Catholic sense of the mass as making present, in sacrament, the sacrifice propitiatory of Jesus Christ on the cross. The intention of preserving the sacrifice that Christ left "unto his faithful" is explicitly stated. Our problem, however, is neither with the exact doctrine of the Anglican reformers nor with the misunderstanding between them and the Catholics concerning eucharistic theology and the language of its formulation. It has to do with the Recusants' judgment on the value of the Ordinal.

Harding is in fact silent on the matter. His rejection of the Edwardine and Elizabethan bishops is not based on a study of the Ordinal, but on a global interpretation of the doctrines and purposes of the reformers, this itself being based on his interpretation of the events that had taken place under Edward VI and at the accession of Elizabeth.

Thomas Stapleton (1535-1598) was probably the most respected Catholic theologian among the Recusants. He was himself not prone to maximize papal authority, and he entertained the delusion that Queen Elizabeth was at heart a good Catholic, who was misled by her advisers! Elizabeth's bishops are only, for him, "the pretended bishops of Protestants"; they have no canonical power, since no one is "left in the realm having authority to consecrate bishops or make priests."[14] Stapleton declares:

> Your pretended bishops have no such ordination as the ancient bishops had, no such laying on of hands of other bishops, no authority to make true priests or ministers, and therefore neither are they any bishops at all.

Nicholas Sanders

Undoubtedly, major theological voices among the Catholic polemicists were entirely in agreement with Harding and Stapleton. In a controversy over the royal supremacy, Nicholas Sanders (c.1530-1581) composed a *De visibili monarchia ecclesiae* (1571) in support of John Feckenham, the deposed abbot of Westminster, against the Anglican bishop of Winchester, Robert Horne (d. 1580). Sanders called Horne "the pseudobishop of Winchester" (*pseudoepiscopum vintoniensem*). This was of course polemical language. And one may wonder if such polemical language was also meant to be theological and doctrinal.

We may turn at this point to the first history of the English Reformation as seen through Recusant eyes. This is, precisely, Nicholas Sanders's *Origins of the Anglican Schism*. Ordained under Henry VIII, in exile under Edward, Sanders became Regius Professor of Canon Law at the University of Oxford under Queen Mary. He took shelter at Louvain under Elizabeth. In 1559 he was in Rome. He attended the diet of Augsburg of 1566 as a theologian in the retinue of the papal legate, Cardinal Comendone. He was called back to Rome by Pius V in 1572. Afer the death of this pope Sanders spent several years in Spain at the court of Philip II. He accompanied the expedition of 1579 to Ireland, where he died. Sanders was one of the best theologians among the Recusants, the author of a remarkable volume on the eucharist, *The Supper of Our Lord* (1565). He also wrote a *Treatise of the Images and of the Saints* (1567), a *Brief Treatise of Usury* (1567), and two defenses of papal authority, *The Rock of Ages* (1567), and *De visibili monarchia ecclesiae* (1571). When he died in 1581 he left an unfinished manuscript in Latin, *De origine ac progressu schismatis anglicanae liber.*

Robert Persons, or Parsons, (1546-1610) was a famous Jesuit who was active in the establishment of the English seminaries of Valladolid, Seville, and St Omer, and for some years directed the seminary in Rome. He was also much involved in the printing of Catholic literature destined to be smuggled into England. He persuaded another priest, Edward Rishton (1550-1585) to finish Sanders's account of the years of Elizabeth. The book came out in Cologne in 1585, and again, with revisions and additions, in 1586. In 1588 a Spanish version, that had been amplified and restructured, was published in Madrid: *Historia Eclesiastica del Cismo del Reino de Inglaterra*. This was the work of Pedro Ribadeneyra (1526-1611), a Spanish Jesuit who had lived in London towards the end of Queen Mary's reign, and had returned to Spain during the first year of Queen Elizabeth.

Three Catholic theologians of value, who had first-hand experience of the times they were describing, who were familiar with both England and Rome, were thus involved in the confection of this history. Their work may therefore be trusted as a gauge of contemporary Catholic reactions to the innovations that were introduced into the Church of England by the English Reformers.

Now, regarding the behavior of the English clergy at the accession of Queen Mary, the *History of the English Schism* has this to say:

> . . . many clerics, who had been ordained schismatically at the time of King Henry and King Edward, with no attention paid to the canons and ecclesiastical laws and without examining by what bishops and how they had been ordained, and whether they were suspended or irregular or tied by

some ecclesiastical censure, with little consideration hastened
to celebrate the sacred mysteries and the divine sacrifice of
the mass. And perchance this was not a minor reason why
this good was lost so fast in that kingdom, by a just punish-
ment from God our Lord, who wants holy things to be
treated with the holiness and reverence that are appropriate,
although later the reconciliation of the kingdom with the
Apostolic See was done, and all received absolution and
blessing (as we shall see), and one should believe that henceforth those who had been so careless wept for their sin with
bitterness and did penance for it.[15]

The author thus bemoans the fact that schismatic priests
proceeded to say the Catholic mass before their official reconciliation with the see of Rome. The schism in question being
that of Henry and of Edward, these clerics had been ordained
indifferently according to the old Pontifical or the Edwardine
Ordinals of 1550 and 1552. The question of the rite is not
raised. There is no hint that the orders may have been invalid,
only that they probably were "irregular," and that the clerics
could have been "suspended" or affected by some other canonical censure. In proper ecclesiastical behavior, they should have
enquired into such a matter before saying mass according to
the Catholic rite. By neglecting this point they "treated the
holy mysteries and the divine sacrifice of the Mass" without
"the proper holiness and reverence." In other words, the central
concern of this passage of the *History of the English Schism* is
canonical rather than theological. It has nothing to do with
the sacrament of orders as such, but only with canonical for-
malities that should have been observed in restoring communion with the Holy See. Concretely, the reconciliation of the
schismatic clergy required an action by a bishop in good standing with the pope. But the clerics, eager to keep their position
under the Catholic queen, anticipated their reconciliation without waiting for an official absolution from censures incurred.

The problem of the marriage of priests is also mentioned.
The bishops of England under Queen Mary ordered the
"priests and religious" who had married

to leave their women, and deprived them of their benefices;

but they admitted them very fast to other and even better benefices; the cause of this was the great penury of priests.[16]

Here also, there is no hint that the married clergy were not priests at all or had been invalidly ordained.

In the matter of the reconciliation of schismatic bishops by the papal legate, the *History of the English Schism* reports the following:

> He confirmed the bishops who had been ordained at the time of the schism, as they were Catholic in their heart, and six other bishops that Henry had, in the same period, instituted again. Although the bishops did not rest satisfied with this general absolution and confirmation, but later each one asked pardon for his fault and special confirmation of his dignity and episcopacy, which they all received benignly from the Apostolic See. There was only one who, more by neglect than by malice, did not seek for this. This was the bishop of Llandaf, who, later, alone of all the bishops, fell again into schism at the time of Queen Elizabeth, and who still lives, that the judgments of God may be seen, noted, and feared.[17]

No distinction is made here between Henrician and Edwardine bishops. They all received confirmation of their episcopate collectively. And only one did not also ask for such a confirmation personally. This was Anthony Kitchin, bishop of Llandaf. Like the priests, the schismatic bishops needed whatever censure they had incurred to be lifted. They also needed confirmation of their episcopal jurisdiction by the Holy See, since whatever authority they had derived only from the royal supremacy, which was, as Thomas More had pointed out to his judges, illegitimate. Yet the matter of validity of ordination is not even raised.

A last text, dealing with the sacrament of confirmation, is relevant. Before the reforms of Vatican Council II, confirmation could normally be received only from bishops. According to the *History of the English Schism,* this sacrament had been extremely popular in England, where it was considered an impiety not to confirm children before they reached seven years of age. The text adds:

And since this sacrament had not been lawfully administered at the time of King Edward, so many were the children
who from all cities, towns, villages and hamlets came to the
bishops to be confirmed, that they could not cope with it,
and sometimes they were in such a crush, on account of the
infinite number of those who came, that it was necessary to
administer it in the fields . . .[18]

This does not suggest that, under Edward VI, confirmation
was not given, or was given by false bishops, or was given
according to an invalid rite. It only states that the sacrament
was not conferred licitly. In other words, the bishops of
Edward VI could effectively confirm, but they could not do so
licitly, for something was lacking in their jurisdiction. Received
from the king by virtue of the royal supremacy, their episcopal
authority was never confirmed by the bishop of Rome. In this
case, a second confirmation was, strictly speaking, superfluous.
It was nonetheless given in answer to popular demand, to
assuage the anxieties of the people. This was in fact the policy
of Cardinal Pole in regard to orders: some priests ordained
during the schism were reordained, not because their first
ordination had been objectively invalid, but in order to allay
their subjective scruples or as a token of repentance. Surprising
as it may seem today, this entailed nothing, in the theology of
the times, regarding the more recent question of invalidity of
orders.

The Problem of Pius V

Elizabeth's aggressive policy against Catholics started in
1570. It was her reaction, that could well have been expected,
to her own excommunication and that of those who would
obey her laws, by Pope Pius V (1566-1572), in the bull *Regnans
in excelsis.*

This bull provides some insight into the Roman outlook on
Anglican orders as these were reorganized in the Elizabethan
settlement. The pope blames the queen for "having followed
and espoused the errors of the heretics." She is only a "pretended queen." The reasons that justify her excommunication
are contained in a series of accusations. Elizabeth has

destroyed the royal council of English nobility, replaced it with obscure heretics, oppressed the followers of the Catholic faith, reestablished dishonest preachers [*concionatores*] and ministers [*administros*] of impieties. She has abolished the sacrifice of the mass, prayers, fasts, the distinction of foods [abstinence], celibacy, and the Catholic rites. She has expelled the bishops, the rectors of churches and the other Catholic priests from their churches and benefices, and has distributed these and other ecclesiastical possessions to heretics . . .[19]

In all this, Pius V does not even suggest that the queen has entrusted bishoprics to false bishops and parishes to false priests. There is no trace of what was later called invalidity of orders. Indeed, the pope asserts that Elizabeth has suppressed "the sacrifice of the mass." But the conclusion that she did not provide for true bishops and priests is not drawn. Instead, the precise thrust of the pope's indictment is that the pretended queen has entrusted the functions of bishops and priests to depraved and heretical men. Pope Pius V did view the Elizabethan bishops and priests as intruders, but he did not systematically regard them as non-ordained or as invalidly ordained. By his time, when there was little chance of a Catholic restoration, the central problem was political rather than theological. Julius III had facilitated the restoration of the clergy, minus their wives: the problem and its solution were disciplinary. Paul IV had destroyed Thomas Cranmer and his pomps and works: the problem and its solution pertained to ecclesiastical politics. Pius V, in a move of last resort, excommunicated the queen and her partisans. By so doing, he released her subjects from all due fealty to their sovereign. In the eyes of papalist lawyers, the queen was thereby made unlawful and her laws and decrees null. In the eyes of legist lawyers, the pope's document had no other civil effect than to incite the queen's subjects to rebellion. The problem and its attempted solution belonged to a political strategy that failed. If Pope Pius thought that this would destroy the queen, he was sorely mistaken. Instead, it nearly destroyed the scattered remnants of the Catholic faithful. Pope Pius was a gambler. In 1571 he would gamble the combined Catholic fleets of the Mediterranean, under the com-

mand of Philip II's half-brother, Don Juan of Austria, against
the Turkish fleet. He would win. In 1570 he gambled his moral
authority against the queen's political authority. The result
was a fiasco.[20]

Conclusion

Harding's position and that of Sanders against the "pseudobishop of Winchester" logically flow from that of Paul IV. Yet
Sanders's language, in his *History of the Schism,* is more
reminiscent of Pope Pius V. The contrast between these points
of view suggests what was the true scope of the question of
orders at the end of the sixteenth century. Officially, the bishops
of Rome did not condemn Anglicans orders or the rite of
ordination of the Ordinal. What they systematically rejected
was the royal supremacy and the authority of those who were
made bishops by virtue of it. The primary question implied in
the matter of Anglican ordinations was, "who ordained?," not,
"what rite was used?" The secondary question was, "how was
that ordainer ordained?"

The theological reason behind the primary importance of
the first question is not far to seek. In the dominant Catholic
school of thought at the end of the Middle Ages, and even to
the eve of Vatican Council II, episcopal power is conveyed,
not by ordination, but by papal confirmation. Sacramentally,
the bishop functions by virtue of the sacrament of orders that
made him a priest. But it is papal confirmation that gives him
the jurisdictional power to act episcopally. Accordingly, when
they substituted the royal supremacy to the papal primacy,
Henry VIII, Edward VI, and Elizabeth removed the effective
source of episcopal authority.

This at least was the Roman view of the matter. With the
one exception of John Fisher (1459-1535), bishop of Rochester,
the bishops of Henry VIII accepted the royal supremacy. They
could appeal to some sorts of precedents. There were the
conciliaristic theologies that had been commonly favored by
the kings of France, and that were still widely shared in the
Christian world, though not in Rome or Spain. Up to 1535,
the bishops of Henry VIII, including Thomas Cranmer, re-

ceived papal confirmation. Those of Edward VI did not. Yet
at the beginning of his reign they were still ordained with the
old Pontifical. Later, after the imposition of the Ordinal by
king and parliament, England was further removed from the
apostolic see, and its rejection of the Roman primacy compounded. In the eyes of Rome, the first could do what the
second could not. With the exception of Kitchin, who in any
case avoided involvement in the politics of the times, the
bishops of Elizabeth were in the same situation as those of
Edward.

The papal documents issued under Mary, Edward, or Elizabeth condemn the royal supremacy and its implications regarding the matter of authority in the Church. They do not
say one clear word about the intrinsic value of the Book of
Common Prayer and of the Ordinal. Outside of a few unordained intruders under Edward VI, the priests of the Church
of England had been ordained either *rite et recte* or *minus rite:*
the first with the old Pontifical, in the *forma ecclesiae consueta,*
the second with the new Ordinals, in a *forma* that the popes of
the sixteenth century never condemn, except insofar as it presupposes the royal supremacy.

Yet Pope Paul IV's time bomb was ticking away. The Recusants who said, "Ye are no bishop!" realized it and drew the
logical conclusion, if at times prematurely. Parker was a true
bishop according to Paul IV's norms, for two of his consecrators, including the main one, had been consecrated according to the Pontifical. But, having himself been made a bishop
by them according to the Ordinal, he would be unable to
ordain any one, even with the Pontifical. And this, of course,
he never did.

Chapter 5

Innocent XI and Clement XI

In modern Catholic canon law, subjective scruples would not provide an acceptable reason for reordination. But the tradition has not been constant on this point. The position of the Eastern Church was ambiguous: priests ordained by "chor-bishops" were often reordained. In the West, the question of reordination was brought up at the beginning of the Donatist controversy, at the time of St. Augustine. Augustine himself extended to the sacrament of orders the previous decision of the Western Church concerning baptism. When conferred by schismatics or heretics who intend "to do what the Church does," these sacraments must not be reiterated. For their author is Christ himself, who acts through the minister. Yet, although the principle was unanimously accepted, the application of this Augustinian theology of sacraments was not constant in the Middle Ages.[1]

The Tradition of Reordination

Many instances could be given. In fact, reordinations were often the rule. The Augustinian interpretation was laid aside when Hincmar of Reims (845-882) denied the value of ordina-tions made by his deposed predecessor, Ebbo (d.851); yet one of these contested priests, Wulfad, was made bishop of Bourges with the approval of Pope Hadrian II. Later, ordinations and consecrations made by Pope Formosus (891-896) were invali-dated by his successors, Sergius III (904-911) and John X

(914-928). Both had been consecrated by Formosus. But as
the installation of the bishop of Rome included an episcopal
consecration, the annulment of Formosus's sacraments was a
way to safeguard their positions as bishops of Rome. For their
second ordination was invalid if the first was valid! Again, in
the long struggle against simony, simoniac ordinations were
generally considered invalid.[2]

Given these precedents, it is hardly surprising that the neat-
ness of Augustine's doctrine did not prevail in the turmoil of
the sixteenth century, when so many non-sacramental points
of view affected the problem of ordination. One should distinguish between two conceptions of the validity of a sacrament. The modern conception is tied to the philosophy and
theology of Counter Reformation scholasticism and, later,
neo-scholasticism. It identifies validity as an inherent metaphysical or ontological quality of an action and its result:
when used according to the rules of the Church, by persons
properly designated for the corresponding function, the ritual
is capable of truly making priests or bishops, by conveying to
them the essence of priesthood or episcopacy.

The older conception was at work through the Middle Ages
and into the early Counter Reformation. It did not touch on
metaphysics or ontology. Whether the ontological reality of
the sacrament and its grace has in fact been given and received
was not the question. The matter was one of recognition.
Invalidity meant invalid in our eyes, not necessarily invalid in
itself. In a certain rite and its use, the Church did, or did not,
recognize what it itself does in the corresponding sacrament.
No judgment was passed on what the Holy Spirit had done or
not done in the ceremony that had taken place. Simply, the
Church, through its lawful authority or magisterium, did or
did not recognize its own action. Whence the power to annul
simoniac ordinations: the Church does not recognize itself in
the selling of sacraments.

That reordinations of clergy and reconfirmations of laity
took place under the authority of the papal legate in England,
Cardinal Pole, is itself sufficiently established.[3] Yet there is
equal evidence that not all were thus reordained or recon-
firmed. Reginald Pole had no qualms using the absolute
powers he had received from Julius III to handle each problem

as it came. Likewise he had no scruple endorsing a reordination or a reconfirmation, if the people involved did not themselves now recognize the sacrament in what they had previously received in a situation of schism.

In these circumstances, it is not surprising that absolute reordinations of Anglican clergy were considered the rule at the end of the seventeenth century and the beginning of the eighteenth. The apostolic letter of Leo XIII cites two precedents, of 1684-85, under Innocent XI (1676-1689), and of 1704, under Clement XI (1700-1721).

The Case of the Anonymous Huguenot

It happened in 1684. A certain French Calvinist sojourned for some time in England. He was ordained a deacon and a priest by the bishop of London. After returning to France he abjured his heresies and was received in the Catholic Church. He did not wish to be a priest. But, when the time came when he wanted to marry, he struggled with scruples. Was he free to marry? Had he in fact received the diaconate and the priesthood? Was he bound by the obligation of celibacy? The case was referred to the Holy Office by the apostolic nuncio in Paris, on July 24, 1684. In his letter, the nuncio delineated the problem as he saw it. One needed to know if the Catholic hierarchy had continued in England despite the national apostasy, and also if, in the Church of England, orders were conveyed through the necessary sacramental form. At the same time, the nuncio's vocabulary suggested what answer he was personally inclined to give to the first question. For he referred, not to the bishops, but to "the pseudo-bishops" of the Church of England.[4]

In 1684, the Counter Reformation was well established on the Continent. In England itself the religious situation was at a difficult point. The king, James II (1633-1701; king, 1685-1688), had become Roman Catholic when, as duke of York, he was exiled in France during the Commonwealth. But he was now contested, both by the Protestant party of the Puritans, who still regretted the restoration of the monarchy, and by moderate Anglicans, who resented the king's open policy of extending to Catholics the same rights to serve in public office that everyone else enjoyed, and the favors he granted to Catholics. Soon, in the "glorious revolution" of 1688, James II would be supplanted by his Protestant daughter, Mary, and her cousin-husband, Prince William of Orange.

Cardinal Jerome Casanate, prefect of the Holy Office, who received the query from Paris, was unaware of the existence of the papal bulls of Julius III and Paul IV. There had been no occasion to refer to them in the past hundred years. They were presumably buried in the dust of the archives. This ignorance of the previous bulls was to have far-reaching consequences. For, as the cardinal could not know the exact scope of the decisions taken in the past, he would have to construct his own problematic independently. He decided to investigate four questions:

(1) How are bishops instituted and consecrated in the Church of England?

(2) Do these consecrated bishops succeed the authentic Catholic bishops of England from before the Reformation?

(3) What are the "form and matter" used in the consecration of bishops?

(4) Is the "matter" sufficient for consecration if the anointing with chrism has been omitted? This question, that is of a more general order than the first three, must have been inspired by the discovery that no chrismation is foreseen in the Ordinal.

The fourth question is easily answered on liturgical and theological grounds: chrismation does not pertain to the essential matter necessary for the consecration of a bishop. The first two questions required historical inquiries.

In his report to a plenary session of the Holy Office, Casanate explained what he had done and what conclusions he had reached. The prefect of the Holy Office had asked for the views of the vicar apostolic of the Netherlands, Bishop Neercassel, and of the internuncio in Flanders, Msgr. Tanari, presumably because these were in frequent contact with exiled English Catholics. Tanari made extensive enquiries among exiled Catholics, and travelled to England on a fact-finding tour, passing on to Rome the information he obtained, including a copy of the Ordinal, both in English and in Latin. The vicar apostolic answered with a long statement, to the effect that he considered the ordinations of the Church of England to be invalid. His negative conclusion was principally based on the idea that "the power of remitting and of retaining sins . . . presupposes the power of sacrificing;" but the Ordinal mentions only the power of "dispensing the sacraments," not that of sacrificing. Since "the form used by the Roman Church" had thus been altered in the Ordinal, Neercassel concluded that the new ritual did not actually contain the necessary form of the sacrament.

Casanate took cognizance of this judgment, of the circumstances of Parker's ordination, and of the prevalent opinion among English Roman Catholics that Parker was not truly a bishop. He examined the Ordinal of 1552 and its revision in 1662. At the restoration under Charles II (1630-1685; king 1660-1685), the Ordinal had been slightly altered. For the king and his advisers wanted to eliminate an interpretation of it that was spreading among the Puritans. As these were opposed to the institution of the episcopate, they argued that the Ordinal did not really make bishops, since the form it used did not mention episcopacy. From then on, the prayer of the Ordinal was more explicit: "Receive the Holy Ghost for the office and work of a bishop . . "

Casanate drew no argument from the suppression of the porrection of the instruments. This, he reported, being inexistent in the Oriental rites, cannot be essential to the conferment of the sacrament of orders. From his enquiries, however, he concluded that the form of the Ordinals of 1552 and 1662 was incapable of conveying the sacrament of order or the episcopate. The apostolic succession was broken when the Catholic form was abandoned. In addition, he considered it more prudent to accept the views of Catholics than those of heretics in so grave a matter. On August 13, 1685, the consultors of the Holy Office voted unanimously that the ordination of the unnamed French Calvinist was not valid. I assume that the petitioner was notified of his freedom to marry. Yet the decision of the Holy Office was never promulgated. It was "delayed" (*dilata*), and never picked up again. Casanate and Clement XI took account of the political difficulties of James II. They were afraid lest publication of a decree declaring Anglican ordinations invalid for lack of the proper form would increase the king's chances of losing his throne.

Be that as it may, Casanate's conclusion may have been correct. It had already been reached by the Elizabethan Recusants. But it was now drawn for different reasons. For the first time in the official documents, the arguments against Anglican orders were taken from what was believed to be the essence of the sacrament. It was the Ordinal as such that was judged incapable of making a priest or a bishop.

The Gordon Case

The case of John Clement Gordon (1644-1726) is more notorious, if not better known, and it is given more space in *Apostolicae curae*. John Gordon was ordained at an unknown date, and no one knows where or with which ritual.[5] He is said to have been a chaplain in the Navy, and he did spend some times in New York, as chaplain for the Anglicans of the city. He was appointed bishop of Galway in Scotland by James II in 1688, after he had rendered some service to the king, most probably as a spy. He was consecrated in Glasgow on September 18, 1688, by the archbishop, James Paterson, and three other bishops. But the rite could not have been, as was assumed in Rome in 1696, the English Ordinal of 1662.

In the first place, Gordon himself provided no information whatsoever about the rite that was used, whether at his ordination or at his consecration. He probably did not know. As a matter of fact, however, the Ordinal of 1662 was not legal in Scotland at the time. What was legal was the Scottish Ordinal of 1620, as revised in 1636. The revision of the Scottish Ordinal had been prompted by Archbishop Laud's critique. Laud was "much troubled," for he felt that the Scottish Ordinal was insufficient: it did not use "the very essential words of conferring Orders." Charles I therefore ordered the Scottish bishops to adopt the formula of the English Ordinal "without change." In other words, Archbishop Laud and King Charles I were satisfied that the Ordinal of 1552 adequately conveyed their own high-church notion of orders and of apostolic succession. But there is no way of knowing if this revised Scottish Ordinal was in fact followed, the Scots being particularly reluctant, partly on patriotic grounds, partly because of the theological turmoil in Scotland, to take their cue from London. It is known that Scottish bishops frequently improvised their liturgy of ordination.

In the second place, whatever could be said about a Scottish ordination was irrelevant to the question of English orders. The authorities in Rome were victims of the confusion of Scotland with England, which is still common today among Continental Europeans. The Roman argument treated Scotland as though it were a province of England, and the Church of Scotland a section of the Church of England. Neither assumption was correct.

There are, in addition, multiple ambiguities about the case. Gordon himself did not stay long in his see. He fled to France at the fall of James II in 1688, when episcopacy was officially abolished in Scotland and the Episcopal Church replaced by the Kirk, which followed Presbyterian polity and Calvinist doctrines. In France he must have frequented the court of James at St-Germain. In 1689 Gordon was in Dublin, where he was made chancellor of the diocese by James II, but he returned to France in 1690, when James put an end to his Irish expedition. It is known that in 1699, when Jacobite restoration had become most unlikely, John Gordon sought rehabilitation in England. Nothing came of it. In 1704, having been widowed for an undetermined number of years, Gordon decided to enter the Catholic Church, apparently under the influence of the famous Bossuet, bishop of Meaux. Shortly thereafter, while sojourning in the city of Rome, Gordon petitioned the Holy See for a judgment on his orders. For Clement XI offered him a benefice for which he had to be at least in minor orders. This benefice is said to have been "the abbey of San Clemente." But San Clemente, in Rome, was not an abbey at the time. There may be another confusion here, coming from the fact that, after his confirmation, Gordon was frequently called, in Italian, *abbate Clemente!* At any rate, Gordon wished to know if he needed to receive these orders, or if he could be presumed to have them already. The minor orders do not exist in the Ordinal. Yet one could entertain the idea that they were received implicitly through ordination to the sacred orders. Gordon's petition, however, was profoundly ambiguous. The petitioner took the position that orders were not validly conferred in the Church of England. The argumentation spoke only of ordination to the episcopate, on the principle, presumably, that if there were no true bishops, there could be no true ordainers. Gordon asked the Holy Office to declare him to be an unordained layman.

There is a touch of irony in the nature of the only two cases touching Anglican ordinations that were submitted to the Holy See between the pontificates of Pius V and of Leo XIII. Neither of the petitioners intended to be a priest in the Catholic Church. The first wished to marry; the second expected a benefice. In either case, a simple dispensation would have been appropriate. That the Holy Office went further in 1684 may be attributed to pastoral solicitude toward the former Calvinist and his scruples about freedom to marry. That no new enquiry was done in 1704 underlines one oddity of *Apostolicae curae,* where it is the extremely ambiguous case of John Gordon, rather than that of the former Huguenot, that is given pride of place. In strict law, this may have been the proper thing to do: since the decision of 1685 had been *dilata,* the case had never been formally closed. The only case where a decision had been finalized was that of the bishop of Galway. But this was a typical instance of double jeopardy. Since there was no certainty as to the rite used at the consecration in Glasgow, whatever was decided had no relevance to the consecration of Matthew Parker! And if the decision was based on the English rite of 1662, it had no relevance to Gordon's Scottish consecration!

A Third Decision?

In the relation he wrote in 1895 for Pope Leo XIII, the Master of the Sacred Palace, Raffaele Pierotti, cited a later act of the Holy Office, occasioned by a complaint of the vicar apostolic of England, Bishop Lawrence Mayes, against an anonymous author's defense of the validity of Anglican orders. The anonymous author was Le Courayer, whose volume, *Dissertation sur la validité des ordinations des Anglois et sur la succession des évêques de l'Eglise anglicane, avec les preuves justificatives des faits avancés,* had been published anonymously in 1723. The complaint was made to the assessor of the Holy Office. On November 27, 1724, the consultors of the Holy Office suggested sending documentation that would contain the previous decisions. On November 29, the members of the Holy Office agreed: the decision of the Gordon case was made known to Mayes.

Pierotti sees in this sending of documentation an authentic interpretation that gave the solution of the Gordon case "maximal and general" value.[9] This, however, seems to be stretching the evidence far beyond the obvious. The point was not retained in *Apostolicae curae.*

The First Theological Debates

Neither the case of the French Calvinist nor the Gordon case attracted the attention of theologians to Anglican orders. Yet discussion of the question has flared up off and on since the second decade of the seventeenth century. The first publication in defense of the Anglican ordinations to the episcopate came from an Anglican pen. Francis Mason's *Of the Consecration of Bishops in the Church of England* was published in London in 1613 (with an expanded edition in Latin in 1625). The book occasioned an extended debate in print.

The theological discussion of Anglican orders entered a new phase when several French theologians joined the fray in the early eighteenth century. What marked this phase was that Roman Catholics were no longer systematically opposed to the value of Anglican ordinations. In 1720 a famous liturgiologist, Abbé Eusèbe Renaudot (1646-1720), published a *Mémoire sur la validité des ordinations des Anglois.* Renaudot did not think that these ordinations could be valid. But he was soon contradicted. A canon of the church of Ste Geneviève in Paris, Pierre Francois Le Courayer (1681-1776), reached the opposite conclusion. His *Dissertation . . .,* that has already been mentioned,[10] was published in Nancy, the capital of the duchy of Lorraine, in 1723, though the title page bore the name of a bookseller in Brussels. During the next few years, Le Courayer and his main contradictor, the Dominican Michel Le Quien (1661-1733), battled back and forth. Le Quien published a lengthy study, *La Nullité des ordinations anglicanes* (2 vol., Paris, 1725). Le Courayer responded with *Défense de la Dissertation . . .* (Brussels, 1726), a book that was successively condemned by the bishops of France and by Pope Benedict XIII (1724-1730), who excommunicated him. Le Quien came back with *La Nullité des ordinations anglicanes démontrée de nouveau contre la Défense du R. P. Le Courayer* (Paris, 1730). Le Courayer responded again with *Supplément aux deux ouvrages faits pour la défense de la validité des ordinations anglicanes* (Amsterdam, 1732).

This last book was written in England, where Le Courayer took refuge after his excommunication in 1728. This excommunication had nothing to do with Anglican orders. Le Courayer was an extreme Gallican. Along with the great patristic scholar, the Oratorian Louis Ellies Dupin (1657-1719) and a few others, he entertained the idea that the Gallican Church ought to achieve a union with the Anglican Church, whether Rome approved or not! He corresponded to that effect with the archbishop of Canterbury, William Wake (1657-1737).[11] Though most of the French bishops shared his Gallicanism to some extent, his advanced thinking, joined to some Jansenist sympathies, did not win their approval. Nevertheless, he never himself joined the Church of England during his long exile.

It is with Le Quien that the distinction begins to be made between erroneous beliefs and doctrines on the part of the consecrator, and even of the authors of the Ordinal, and perverse intent in eliminating specific doctrines from the Ordinal. The first do not affect the validity of the sacrament conferred. The second, for Le Quien, does: "The prayer must express what the faith teaches us about the Sacrament of Order; it must mention the Priesthood in relation to the Sacrifice which is its main function . . ."[12] Why this should be so, however, is not adequately explained.

Conclusion

One point is well illustrated by the episodes of 1684 and 1704. The problem of the sixteenth century was no longer that of the late seventeenth and early eighteenth centuries. Neither Julius III nor Paul IV had considered the measures taken by Cardinal Pole on their general instructions as settling anything at the level of the essence of the sacrament of orders. The problem that Julius III was eager to solve was that of clerical celibacy, and what to do with the married clergy after the reign of Edward VI. As to Paul IV's main concern, it was the royal supremacy itself, its impact in England, and its possible repercussions in other lands. He wanted to counterbalance the deplorable example that kings had been given by the English sovereigns. For there were some who, while Catholic in faith and doctrine, might be attracted to similar antipapal measures.

When the case of the former French Calvinist was examined, Rome could not forget the Pragmatic Sanction of Charles VII of France. Louis XIV was reigning. He approved of the "Four Articles of the Gallican Clergy concerning ecclesiastical authority," that had been proclaimed by the Assembly of the Clergy on March 19, 1682. The Four Articles limited papal authority within the French kingdom. No less a bishop than the great Bossuet, whose influence at the court of Louis XIV was considerable, had taken an active part in their adoption.[13] (His long *Defensio declarationis cleri gallicani de ecclesiastica potestate* was to be published posthumously.) Neither Louis XIV nor Bossuet entertained the idea of a schism. Yet Rome could not be too cautious.

Meanwhile, the scholasticism of the Counter Reformation was fast abandoning the spirit of medieval theology. The Catholic Church, especially in its hierarchy, was seen as the image of heavenly power. Sacraments were more and more approached in terms of their essence. Functional theology was being drowned under a wave of metaphysical statements. "Catholic truth," Bossuet wrote, "has its perfection at the beginning."[14] On this point at least the Jansenists agreed with him. But if Catholic doctrine is perfect from the beginning, then any later alteration of its doctrines, as in Protestantism, and of the liturgies that embody the doctrines, as in Anglicanism, is less than perfect. It is a defect, a threat to the fulness of Catholicism, an attempt to dismantle and ruin its imposing edifice.

Thus it was that the events of 1550, 1552, and 1559 were

seen under a different light a century and a half later than at
the time of their happening. The popes who struggled with the
situation created by Henry VIII, Edward VI, and Elizabeth
were still functioning with a largely medieval frame of reference. It is the Church as a whole and the general framework of
its liturgy that give the tone of the sacramental acts, and are
indicative of their meaning. That the ordaining bishops intend
to do what the Church does is taken for granted. The cue to
their intention does not lie strictly in the words they use and
the gestures they do. It is provided by their fidelity to the
Church as the universal Communion of the faithful. Before
1570 it was debatable to what extent the Church in England
was no longer in the Communion. The requirements imposed
by Julius III for reconciliation were minimal. Paul IV, being
primarily anxious about royal supremacy and papal authority,
refused to recognize the acts of the Edwardine bishops. But he
drew from his negative stance no metaphysical conclusions
concerning the nature or essence of the sacrament of orders
and the theoretical capability of the Ordinal to serve as an
instrument to do what the Church does.

One century later the mentalities had changed, along with
the way of doing theology. The scholasticism of the Counter
Reformation was reigning. The Jansenist controversies, that
started shortly after 1630 with the publication of Cornelius
Jansen's *Augustinus,* had prompted doctrinal debates on the
metaphysics of grace. The quarrel between Dominicans and
Jesuits over the means of grace (*auxilia gratiae*), begun in the
late sixteenth century, had led to theological speculation on
the nature of created grace. The silence imposed on the two
parties by Paul V in 1611 and Urban VIII in 1625 and 1641 did
not quench the ambition of theologians to arrive at absolutely
certain ontological conclusions. The controversy over quietism
followed the same direction. Michael Molinos was condemned
in 1682, by Innocent XI, and Fénelon's volume, *L'Explication
des Maximes des saints sur la vie intérieure,* published in 1697,
was condemned in 1699. The feeling was abroad that one
could define the essence of Christian holiness. Like the churches of the Baroque style, the theologies were monuments that
embraced, or tried to embrace, all religious knowledge. They
reached to the metaphysics of the spiritual and the sacramental.

In these conditions, the research initiated by Cardinal Casanate inspired a conclusion that was out of proportion to the question. Pope Innocent XI may well have wished simply to assuage the scruples of a convert and to facilitate the task of the Catholic King James II. On the one hand, neither he nor Clement XI had urgent questions to answer regarding orders in the *Ecclesia anglicana*. On the other, the popes had now no control over the politics of England: whatever would happen in London would result from political and military actions taken in England, not from theological decisions made in Rome. But the conclusion reached by the prefect of the Holy Office was more important than it seems at face value. For it would now be integrated in a general tractate on the sacramental system. This was precisely the point at stake between Le Courayer and Le Quien: does history tell us if the essence of the sacrament of orders was preserved through the English Reformation? The problem of Anglican orders now touched the *esse* of the sixth sacrament. This was no longer the same question as in the sixteenth century.

Chapter 6

Leo XIII (I)

This is not the place to examine in detail the process by which the question of Anglican orders was brought to the attention of Pope Leo XIII (1878-1903). The story has been told at length several times.[1] The impetus came from the "unionist" endeavors of a distinguished Anglican layman, Charles Linsley Wood, second Viscount Halifax (1839-1934), and his Roman Catholic friend, Fernand Portal (1855-1926), a priest in the Vincentian Order. In a word, they hoped that the pope would recognize Anglican orders, and that this would hasten the reconciliation of Rome and Canterbury.

In this connection many researches would be appropriate, that need not be done at this point. It would be legitimate, but beyond the scope of the present review, to enquire into the methodology adopted by the advisory commission appointed by the pope, into the direct or indirect pressures that the Catholic bishops of England, and especially the archbishop of Westminster, Cardinal Herbert Vaughn (1832-1903, archbishop in 1892), may have brought to bear on the pope, into the lobbying role played by the personage who acted as the English bishops' agent in Rome, the future cardinal Rafael Merry del Val (1865-1930).

Yet some preliminary considerations will help to estimate the nature and to gauge the scope of Pope Leo's apostolic letter of 1896, *Apostolicae curae*.

The Intellectual Context

Comparative studies of the official texts of separated

Churches had been initiated in 1832 by the great German Catholic theologian, Johann Adam Moehler (1796-1838), in his book, *Symbolics*. This was an investigation of the similarities and dissimilarities between the decrees of the council of Trent and the Confessional Books of the Lutheran Churches. It was neither by design nor by accident that the study of Anglican orders took the form of a comparison between the Anglican Ordinal and the Catholic Pontifical. Simply, the theological mood and fashion inclined in that direction.

Such an investigation, led in Rome by Catholic authors, suffered from a prejudice in favor of centralization and uniformity. Before the French Revolution many local usages in the liturgical services of the Catholic dioceses of Europe were accepted without question. During the Revolution the Civil Constitution of the Clergy, imposed by the Constituent Assembly in 1790, was based on conciliaristic and Gallican principles, which preserved the liturgies but reduced papal authority to a bare minimum. With the reorganization of the nation by Napoleon, the restoration of the Catholic Church followed the centralizing trend that was favored by the emperor. Dom Guéranger, who reestablished the Benedictine Order at Solesmes, entertained the novel idea that the forms of liturgy should be the same everywhere. Diversity in worship was believed to promote Gallicanism in ecclesiastical politics. Few of the local rites of France survived the reforms advocated by Guéranger, and these served as the basic model for the Catholic Church as a whole. Uniformity was brought to the forms of worship by giving primacy to the liturgy of Rome over local customs. In so doing, the Church naturally reinforced the centralizing lines of the papal primacy. This movement culminated in the proclamation of papal infallibility in 1870, at Vatican Council I.

In these conditions it was inevitable that the growing centralization of the Catholic Church should bring suspicion on other than the standard rites. When therefore Pope Leo XIII was asked to express his judgment on the efficacy of Anglican ordinations, the minds of Roman theologians were not generally open toward whatever rites were not in conformity with actual Roman usage. Although nobody noticed it at the time, and least of all those who brought the matter to Pope Leo's attention, the dice were already loaded against the recognition of Anglican orders by the Catholic hierarchy.

Another cultural phenomenon, peculiar to the nineteenth century, was likely to influence Leo XIII and his advisers. This was the growing influence of scientism and the belief that the scientific method has an absolute value and leads to unimpeachable conclusions. The myth of the unhampered march of scientific progress was so pervading that one school of historians began to consider history an absolute science. Jules Michelet really believed that he constructed authentic images of the past through his imaginative interpretation of events and documents. It therefore seemed natural to think that a historical investigation of the documents illustrating the sixteenth century in England would be able to construct so exact a picture of the events of the times, that the pope could arrive at an absolute conclusion, and that he would be able to answer with certainty the question, "Are Anglican orders valid or invalid?" Admittedly, under the guidance of Pius IX, the Roman Church had reacted against the scientific and philosophical trends of the period, notably at Vatican Council I. Church historians were hardly contaminated by scientism. Msgr Duchesne, the most learned historian on Pope Leo's Commission, had a sanely modest view of the achievements of historical research. The most popular history of the Catholic Church was, throughout the nineteenth century, the *Annals* of Baronius, which, revised and updated by subsequent authors, antedated the growth of scientism. Still, one cannot rule out that churchmen, who were not themselves practitioners of historical research, could be affected by the belief that absolute historical conclusions were within reach, provided sufficient documentation were available. Contemporary historians are less sanguine about the human capacity to obtain an unbiased absolute certainty about the structure of past events and their motivations and purposes.

The Fear of Contamination

Early in the long pontificate of Pius IX (1846-1878) the attention of the Roman curia was drawn to English and

Anglican matters. In July 1844, an English Passionist, Ignatius Spencer, while preaching and lecturing in Belgium, had launched a campaign of prayers for the conversion of England, for which he enlisted a number of nunneries. The Oxford Movement and the conversion of John Henry Newman in 1845 had occasioned a great deal of interest, especially in France. The concern for the unity of the Church was coming to the fore in Catholic preoccupations. In 1857, an English Catholic layman, Ambrose Phillips de Lisle, and an Anglican clergyman, Frederick George Lee, had founded an Association for the Promotion of the Unity of Christendom.[2] But was it prudent to let Catholic laity and clergy join with Anglicans in such a project?

For the Roman mind, the problem was new. The pre-ecumenical period of what has been called "unionism" had not yet appeared on the horizon. It is therefore not surprising that the official response, inspired by pastoral, if somewhat excessive, caution, was negative. The letter of the Holy Office, *Ad omnes episcopos Angliae* (September 16, 1864), urged the restored Roman Catholic hierarchy of England not to favor the activities of this organization. Later, the prefect of the Holy Office, Cardinal Patrizi, defended this cautious position in an answer to a petition signed by one hundred and ninety-eight Anglican clergymen: *Ad quosdam Puseistas Anglicos* (November 8, 1865).[3]

The Neo-scholastic Method

In the last decades of the nineteenth century the Catholic Church was still emerging from the trauma of the French Revolution. This was especially true in regard to the intellectual life. The Revolution had brought to an end the university system inherited from the Middle Ages. In the new universities established by Napoleon, and imitated in most Continental nations, theology was no longer the queen of knowledge. Led by Pope Pius IX (1846-1878), Vatican Council I, in 1870, had reaffirmed the capacity of the human reason to know, to know the morality implied in the natural law, and even to know God's existence and basic attributes as reflected in the created world.[4] In 1879 Pope Leo himself had placed, as it were, the keystone in the vault of the new Catholic cathedral of learning. He had affirmed the normative strength of scholasticism in general and of Thomism in particular, as regards both philosophy and theology (encyclical *Aeterni Patris*). The outcome of this choice of an intellectual model for Catholic thought was the growth and eventual predominance—for a time— of a new, modernized, form of scholasticism. In these conditions, it was inevitable that Leo's point of view regarding sacraments would be inspired by Thomas Aquinas. Yet the common doctor was read and understood in the light of the great commentators of the Counter Reformation rather than in the context of medieval pluralism.

Moreover, several nineteenth-century Catholic authors had already studied Anglican orders. The off and on discussion of the topic, that had surfaced from time to time in previous centuries, had flared up again in the 1840's.

The Judgment of Peter Kenrick

One may wonder at this point to what extent the argumentation of *Apostolicae curae* could be original. The discussion of the validity of Anglican orders by Catholic authors was by no means a new thing when the question was brought to pope Leo's attention by Lord Halifax and Monsieur Portal. Among the works that were then recent one finds a belated refutation of Le Courayer by Peter Kenrick (1806-1893), who, as archbishop of St Louis, was to be in the anti-infallibilist minority at Vatican Council I: *The Validity of Anglican Ordinations and Anglican Claims to Apostolical Succession Examined* (Philadelphia, 1841).

After describing the state of the question (ch. 1), Kenrick explains "the sentiments of English Reformers regarding Ordination" (ch. 2) and the denial of validity to the consecration of Anglican bishops by the Elizabethan Recusants (ch. 3). The central part of the book examines three aspects of the question: Parker's consecration (ch. 4); Barlow's consecration (ch. 5); "the validity of Edward's Ordinal" (ch. 6). Ch. 4 and 5 are a detailed discussion of legal or alleged documents tending to prove, first, that the record of Parker's consecration in the Lambeth Register was a forgery, second, that Parker was not consecrated on December 17, 1559, and third, that, along with others, Parker's main consecrator, William Barlow, bishop-elect of Chichester and former bishop of St David's, had never himself been consecrated (ch. 5). In addition, Kenrick maintains that the Nag's Head story, if possibly not entirely true, has a good deal of likelihood. The Nag's Head, Kenrick believes, was an inn for clergy. It had a chapel, in which it would not have been improper for an ordination to take place (ch. 7).

None of this would be relevant to a discussion of *Apostolicae curae,* were it not for the examination of the Ordinal (ch. 6). This turns around five points, that are neatly summed up by Kenrick:

> First. The change of the form was an act of the civil power, and the forms thus introduced derive their authority from no other source.
>
> Second. The change was made for the purposes of accommodating the rite to the opinions then entertained by the promoters of the English Reformation, and of destroying the notions which, before such change, were attached to the words, priest and bishop.
>
> Third. The change made was such as to leave no expression of the power of priest and bishop, even in the sense in which these words are taken by that division of Anglicans who are known to entertain High Church principles, and the form so changed is essentially different from those which are used in the Churches, the ordinations of which are regarded as valid.
>
> Fourth. The change of form, made by Convocation in 1662, is a satisfactory proof of the insufficiency of the form originally devised by Edward VI.
>
> Fifth. The Roman Catholic church has, from the beginning, uniformly condemned the ordinations of the Church of England as invalid, and this rejection is grounded, principally, on the defective form employed in such ordinations.[5]

Now, point 2 corresponds to *Apostolicae curae* on the *nativa indoles ac spiritus* of the Ordinal, point 3 to its argument on "defect of form," point 4 to its erroneous view of the addition made in 1662, point 5 to the argument from precedent. One may suspect that the actual writer of the apostolic letter was acquainted with, and possibly influenced by, Kenrick's volume. This may well be the reason why a rejection of the Nag's Head fable was included in *Apostolicae curae*. At any rate, *Apostolicae curae* explicitly disclaimed any trust in the Nag's Head story. And it drew no argument from the contention that Barlow was not a bishop of all. This denial of Barlow' episcopacy rested on the fact that the register of Barlow's consecration had not been found in the archives. But Henry VIII, who was strict in such matters, would not have tolerated that a non-bishop function as a bishop!

The Judgment of Franzelin

A book on Anglican orders was published in London in 1873 by an English Roman Catholic, Canon E.E. Estcourt: *The Question of Anglican Ordinations Discussed*. In this volume, Estcourt accepted the principle that the Ordinal's form of ordination was not absolutely defective in itself. In the right hands, it could express the intention to do what the Church does. Estcourt, however, believed that the English form was not used with that intention and in an orthodox sense by the consecrators of Matthew Parker. The source of the defect in Anglican ordinations was not an *intentio faciendi,* but an *intentio circa significationem,* that is, not an intention regarding the action performed (the ordination), but an intention regarding the meaning of this action.[6] This intention was tied to the early Anglican (Zwinglian) doctrine of the eucharist and the mass. The bishops of Elizabeth positively excluded making "sacrificing priests," and in so doing they excluded doing what the Church does.

In this book, Estcourt discussed the relevance of an answer believed to have been given in 1704 by the Holy Office concerning a defect in ordinations made in the Coptic Church of Abyssinia. The Holy Office would have responded that the defect was not such as to invalidate the ordinations. In 1875, the archbishop of Westminster, Cardinal Henry Manning

(1808-1892), himself a former Anglican priest, inquired of the Holy Office whether the decision of 1704 concerning Abyssinian orders was applicable to Anglican orders. The answer was given on April 30, 1875, by the prefect, Cardinal Patrizi. The decision of 1704 was in fact not a decree. It was only the opinion of a consultor. And in any case it had no implications bearing on Anglican orders.

Now, the distinguished German theologian Johann Baptist Franzelin (1816-1886) had been consulted on this point by Cardinal Patrizi.[7] His memorandum had taken a close look at the ritual of Anglican ordinations. The question, for Franzelin, was whether "the Catholic form of ordination was changed essentially into another rite with another and divergent meaning." Against Estcourt, Franzelin considered the consecrator's "intention in regard to meaning" to be irrelevant. The key lay only in the actual words of the formula of ordination and their meaning, that is, in the scholastic "form." It is Franzelin's judgment that, under Edward VI, "the external rite itself was wholly changed, the Catholic rite was repudiated, and a new one adopted with publicly professed heresy, with the aim of deleting from the rite all that signified the priestly power, which is the power of consecrating and offering the sacrifice of the New Testament."[8] Accordingly, it makes no difference whether somewhere else, in other circumstances, the rite could have a Catholic sense. In the Ordinal it has only a heretical sense. It is therefore incapable of conveying the true priesthood intended by Christ.

This is so close to Leo XIII's conclusion that the dependence of *Apostolicae curae* on Franzelin's memorandum is virtually certain.

Leo XIII's Commission

By the beginning of 1896, a number of Catholic theologians had expressed or were expressing their views on Anglican orders. The catalyst that brought the question to a head was Portal's own publication, issued under a pen name, F. Dalbus: *Les Ordinations anglicanes* (Arras, 1894). In this provocative volume, which he himself gave Pope Leo, Portal argued for the probable invalidity of Anglican orders on the basis of the absence of the porrection of instruments in the rite of the Ordinal. This argument was so weak that the validity of the orders appeared to be the proper conclusion!

As Leo wished for more information, he had recourse to some well known professors. In October 1894 the French historian, Msgr. Louis Duchesne, was invited by the nuncio in Paris (who had received instructions from the secretary of State, Cardinal Rampolla) to make a study of Anglican orders. The result was Duchesne's *Mémoire sur les ordinations anglicanes,* of December 1894. Duchesne concluded that, while the ritual of ordination to the diaconate was quite insufficient, the rituals of ordination to the priesthood and to the episcopate were sufficient. Since Duchesne was primarily a historian, known for his study of *Les Origines du culte chrétien* (published in 1889), his main point of reference was taken from the early rites of ordination. In addition, an Italian theologian and canon lawyer, Pietro Gasparri, who was at the time teaching in Paris, was asked for his views by Cardinal Galimberti. Previously, in a book on sacraments, Gasparri had uncritically accepted the Nag's Head story. He now discovered that this was pure fable. His booklet, *De la Valeur des ordinations anglicanes,* was printed in Rome in October 1894 and distributed to the members of the Holy Office. It was published in Paris in 1895. Gasparri concluded that Anglican converts could be ordained conditionally: while their ordination was probably valid, there remained a reasonable doubt in regard to both form and intention. Finally, the Italian Jesuit, Emilio De Augustinis, was also invited by Pope Leo to express his views. For some fourteen years De Augustinis had taught dogmatic theology, including courses on the sacraments, at the American scholasticate of Woodstock (Maryland). In 1894 he held the chair of dogmatics at the Collegio Romano, in Rome itself. He composed a memorandum, *Sulla Validità delle Ordinazioni Anglicane,* in August 1895. He concluded to the validity of the ordinations.

As this was going on, an English commission was set up by Cardinal Vaughn in 1895. It finalized its negative conclusions in a report issued on March 12, 1896: *Ordines Anglicani. Expositio historica et theologica.* Anglican orders are null, and convert Anglican clergy must never be ordained *sub con-*

ditione, but *absolute.* The authors of this report were Canon
James Moyes, Dom Adrian Gasquet, and the Franciscan
David Fleming. Moyes had authored thirty-one articles on
Anglican orders that were published in *The Tablet* between
February and December, 1895, and he was to write nineteen
more after the publication of *Apostolicae curae.* Gasquet was
a historian, whose major work had been done in collaboration
with another scholar, Edmund Bishop.

These six authors were named by Leo XIII to the Commission for the study of Anglican orders. The president was Cardinal Marcello Mazzella, De Augustinis's predecessor in the
chair of dogmatic theology at the Collegio Romano. However,
the secretary was no other than Cardinal Vaughn's informant
in Rome, Rafael Merry del Val, who was adamantly opposed
to the validity of Anglican orders. Two other members were
added after the first meeting. One was a parish priest, T.B.
Scannell. In six letters printed in *The Tablet,* Scannell had
taken the position that the matter of Anglican ordinations was
not settled by Paul IV, whose bull, *Regimini universalis ecclesiae,* had recently been rediscovered. Scannell had been recommended by Baron Von Hügel in a communication to
Cardinal Rampolla: *Mémoire adressé par ordre à Son Emi-
nence le cardinal Rampolla, sur les rapports entre les catholiques Anglais et les Anglicans* (December 15, 1895). To balance
Scannell's influence, however, a known opponent of the
validity of Anglican orders was also named, the Spaniard
Calasanzio de Llaveneras, consultor to the Holy Office.[9]

The Commission met twelve times, from March 24 to May
5, 1896. Given its membership and the personality of its secretary, it could reach no conclusion. All its documentation was
eventually placed in the hands of the Dominican Raffaele
Pierotti. As Master of the Sacred Palace, Pierotti was told by
Leo XIII to sum up the Commission's work. He was then to
present his findings to the members of the Holy Office, who
would make a formal recommendation to the pope.

The pro . . .

Duchesne's paper examines four points:[10] (1) the facts: were

Parker and Barlow actually consecrated to the episcopate? (2) the rite: is the Anglican Ordinal sufficient? (3) the intention, and (4) the origin of the practice of reordination. Duchesne's answers are easily summed up: (1) Parker and Barlow were certainly consecrated; (2) the form of the Ordinal is as sufficient as many Oriental forms, that are not more explicit than it is about the tasks of a priest and of a bishop, though it is insufficient in regard to the diaconate; the difference with the Roman form is only one of degree; (3) Cranmer in composing the Ordinal, and the Anglican bishops in using it, intend to do what the Church does; (4) the Roman practice of absolute ordination for Anglican converts does not imply the invalidity of the Anglican form, for reordinations of priests and bishops ordained according to an unquestioned form have been frequent at several periods of Church history.

While Duchesne was more a historian than a theologian, it was the reverse with De Augustinis.[11] The latter's report of course discusses the salient historical points, but its strength lies in the author's theological reflections. It is in two parts. (1) The first shows that the Holy See has never yet made a pronouncement on the value of Anglican ordinations. In 1685 the Holy Office appended the word, *Dilata,* to its finding regarding the former Calvinist: this means that the decision on the substance of the question was delayed indefinitely. In 1704, the solution of the Gordon case implicitly rejected Gordon's tendentious or false arguments against the validity of his orders. In 1555, Paul IV, as well as Cardinal Pole, avoided touching the fundamental question of the essential value of the Ordinal. (2) In the second part, De Augustinis argues that in 1559 Matthew Parker was validly consecrated a bishop (§1): his consecrators had the power to do it (§2); they used a rite that had been doctored but remained valid, for it preserved the two elements that are necessary for ordination, a laying on of hands by bishops and a consecratory prayer that conveys the sense of what is being done (§3); the consecrators' intention was to do what the Church does (§4).

De Augustinis maintains that the heresies of Cranmer concerning the eucharist and the Church are irrelevant. For the constant Catholic doctrine has been that it is Christ who gives the grace of the sacrament, and that Christ's action is not hindered by the minister's sins or heresies. This was made clear in the decisions of the Fathers concerning baptism given by the Arians. It is abundantly affirmed and explained in the theologies of Thomas Aquinas and of Bellarmine: the minister "acts in the person of the whole Church, from whose faith what is lacking in the minister's faith is supplied."[12] Supposing that the consecrators had the explicit intention of doing, not what the Church of Rome does, but only what the Church of England does, even this would not affect the result. For, in Bellarmine's words, "The minister's error concerning the Church does not nullify the efficacy of the sacrament; only defect of intention does."[13] And there can be no defect of intention as long as the minister intends to do what Christ does in the action of his true Church. The minister's mistake as to what Christ does, or as to the identity of the Church, has itself no effect, for the intention that is required bears "on what the Church does, not on what the Church intends to do,"or on what the Church is.

. . . and the con

As presented at the time of Pope Leo's Commission, the case against Anglican orders took two forms, one emotional, the other theological.

The emotional case can be illustrated from a reminder of the conviction shared by the Roman Catholic bishops of England that Cardinal Vaughn sent to Cardinal Mazzella on May 10, 1896. This took the form of a letter sent by him in the name of all the bishops of England and Wales.[14] It was accompanied by letters of support, that Vaughn had solicited from the bishops of Scotland and Ireland. Vaughn's letter was a disingenuous document. It showed both a ferocious determination to stop any recognition of Anglican orders, and a great ignorance of the theological mood within the Church of England past and present. Seven points were made by the archbishop of Westminster: (1) The "honor of Our Lord in the Blessed Sacrament," and (2) that of the sacrament of penance, "demand" the condemnation of Anglican orders. (3) The opposite decision would "keep Anglicans in their heresy." (4) Machiavellian motivations are attributed to High Church leaders:

their aim is to set up "a Catholic Church which is independent of Rome and in rivalry with it," and that "would be the head of the Anglo-Saxon or English-speaking races throughout the world, as Rome is of the Latin races." (5) Furthermore, all in England, Protestant and Catholic, agree that a corporate reunion is out of the question. (6) Yet "the Archbishops and the mass of Protestants" encourage Lord Halifax, because they would gain something from approval of the Ordinal or from a change of Roman policy in favor of the ordination *sub conditione* of convert Anglican clergy. (7) Finally, condemnation will "disappoint the High Church party" and bring about an influx of conversions among those Anglicans who wish to have valid orders.

Intentional or coincidental, this delusion about the happy effects to be expected from a condemnation was supported by the timely spread of a pamphlet in Italian, *Risposta all' Opusculo 'De Re Anglicana.'* Printed in Rome in 1896, this was the work of Gasquet and Moyes. The authors refuted another pamphlet, in Latin, *De Re Anglicana,* recently printed in Rome by an Anglican scholar, T.A. Lacey.[15] At the suggestion of Cardinal Rampolla himself, Lacey was lingering in Rome with his friend Portal and another Anglican, F.W. Puller. The secretary of State thought that members of the Commission might wish to consult with them on the historical aspects of the question. In May, Lacey had published in England *Dissertationes apologeticae de Hierarchia Anglicana.* Issued in Rome a short time later, *De Re Anglicana* complemented the picture by explaining the English scene. In it Lacey described the nature and comprehensiveness of the Church of England.

The *Risposta* was filled with bitter accusations against Lacey in particular and Anglicans in general. It presented a very hostile picture of the English Reformation. It was especially virulent against the Anglo-Catholics, among whom the Oxford movement of Keble, Pusey, and the early Newman was still bearing fruit within the Church of England. It even made statements that were manifestly untrue, as for instance that the average Anglican parish celebrates the eucharist only once a month.

What deserves to be remembered, however, is not the authors' polemical exaggerations. It is their emotional appeal. They see the devil at work in the Anglo-Catholic movement. They paint a glowing picture of the happy results to be expected from a condemnation of Anglican orders: "There is no doubt that the already large number of converts will increase if it is made more evident that the Roman Catholic Church is the only one in England which has a right to the prerogatives and name of *Catholic*."[16] This line of thought could hardly be dismissed by a pastorally-minded pope, who lived before the start of the ecumenical movement.

The Master of the Sacred Palace

The theological case against the validity of Anglican orders was presented to Leo XIII by Raffaele Pierotti.[17] Traditionally, the Master of the Sacred Palace has acted as the pope's private theological adviser. Having in hand all the documentation available to the Commission, and all necessary information as to the tenor of its debates, Pierotti reached his own conclusion, that he formulated in his *Voto sulle Ordinazioni Anglicane,* which bears the date, May 28, 1896. Limiting himself to the key question of ordination to the episcopate, Pierotti surveyed the historical evidence from the sixteenth century, the reviews of the matter in 1685-86 and in 1704, and the debates in the Commission. His conclusion, however, was evidently based on his personal theology. Pierotti held to a rigid conception of sacramental form: since it is from the form that the matter of a sacrament obtains its meaning, and the sacrament itself its nature, the form must clearly identify the sacrament in question. This is, for Pierotti, required for validity: "It is necessary to the validity of episcopal consecration that the form specify the order or power (*ordinem seu potestatem*) that is being conferred."[18] Pierotti therefore concluded that Anglican consecrations to the episcopate are invalid for "lack of the due form and of the due intention."[19] He added that a "new solemn, formal, and explicit" condemnation of Anglican orders, based on defect of form and defect of intention, was both necessary and opportune.

In favor of the opportunity of such a condemnation Pierotti

cited the *votum* that a certain professor Fejie, consultor to the Holy Office, had formulated during the preparation of Vatican Council I, in 1868: because "Anglican ordinations are null and void (*nullae et irritae*), the Anglican bishops as such must be ignored" in the invitations to the council.[20] And a condemnation of Anglican orders by the council will bring such vast numbers of Anglican priests and laity to conversion that the reunion of the Church of England will take place, despite the Anglican bishops, at the end of the council! Vatican I, of course, took no such step. And conversions from Canterbury to Rome have never been more than a trickle! It is indeed curious that this did not alert the Roman Catholic bishops of England, and Pierotti himself, to the fallacy of this whole approach!

Be that as it may, the vote of the members of the Holy Office could not come as a surprise. On Thursday, July 16, they met in the presence of the pope. They voted unanimously that Anglican orders were not valid. One member, however, did not attend the meeting. This was no less a person than the secretary of State, Cardinal Mariano Rampolla del Tindaro (1843-1913). There is a strong presumption that Rampolla did not favor the condemnation of Anglican orders.

The Relevance of Satis cognitum

Leo XIII was himself deeply concerned about matters of Christian unity. Apart from the various documents he published relating to the Oriental Churches and from several letters addressed by himself and by his curia to the English nation,[21] he issued a major encyclical on the general question of the unity of all Christians. *Satis cognitum* came out on June 20, 1896, less than three months before *Apostolicae curae* (September 13). The encyclical sees unity along the lines of what has been called "unionism," rather than of the more recent ecumenism that was endorsed at Vatican Council II.[22] The ecclesiology is of course centralizing and ultramontane. There is no need to review its presentation of the "center of unity" in Peter and Peter's successors. Yet two points that are made in *Satis cognitum* are directly relevant to the concerns of

Apostolicae curae.

The first is a strong endorsement of the inseparability of the different Christian doctrines. All that is taught by the magisterium as "contained in the deposit of divine revelation must be believed by every one as true." The doctrines belong together. Rejecting one is tantamount to rejecting all:

> In this wise, all cause for doubting being removed, can it be lawful for any one to reject one of those truths without by the very fact falling into heresy? without separating himself from the Church? without repudiating in one sweeping act the whole of Christian teaching? For such is the nature of faith that nothing can be more absurd than to accept some things and reject others.[23]

Under the name of "analogy of faith," this principle had already been incorporated in Leo XIII's encyclical on biblical studies, *Providentissimus Deus,* of November 18, 1893. It manifestly was an important axiom in the pope's theological method.

The second point is the description of the sorry state of bishops separated from the see of Peter:

> From this it must be clearly understood that bishops are deprived of the right and power of ruling, if they deliberately secede from Peter and his successors; because, by this secession, they are separated from the foundation on which the whole edifice must rest. They are therefore outside the *edifice* itself; and for this very reason they are separated from the *fold,* whose leader is the chief Pastor; they are exiled from the *Kingdom,* the keys of which were given by Christ to Peter alone.[24]

These two points are closely related to the reasoning of *Apostolicae curae.* The first implies that rejection of one doctrine entails the rejection of all the faith. The second betrays Leo's secret hope that Cardinal Vaughn was right: awed by the realization of their shepherdless state, the Anglican faithful should logically knock at the gate of the true sheepfold!

Leo XIII himself was genuinely concerned about the state of religion in England. This interest was not unrelated to his study of the social problems of modern industrial society, that was illustrated by the encyclicals, *Immortale Dei* (on modern society, 1885), *Libertas praestantissimum* (on liberty and freedom of conscience, 1888), and *Rerum novarum* (on social questions, 1891). England was at the advanced point of industrial progress. At the same time, the position of the Catholic majority in Ireland, that was still part of the United Kingdom, had reached a dangerous point. The movement for Irish emancipation, favored by the people, was not supported by the hierarchy. The bishops actively opposed the parliamentary leader of the movement for emancipation, Stewart Parnell (1846-1891), who was both an Anglican and a divorced man! In the circumstances, anything Rome might say relating to Roman Catholicism in the British Isles was believed to be touchy.

Be that as it may, Leo had listened to a suggestion made by Portal and supported by Halifax, and to which Cardinal Vaughn was not opposed. He issued an appeal to the people of England, the apostolic letter *Amantissimae voluntatis,* often called, the letter *Ad Anglos* ("To the English"), of April 14, 1895. Though the letter was addressed directly to Cardinal Vaughn only, it intended to reach all those in England who "seek the kingdom of Christ in unity of faith." It was warm in its tone, but vague in its references, as it made no mention of the Church of England or any of the Protestant Churches. Yet the letter was generally welcome.[25] Both the political "liberal" leader, Gladstone, and the archbishop of York acknowledged it. Its immediate result, however, did not materialize in London, but in Paris. Fernand Portal founded an "Association for the Reunion of the Anglican Church," and a magazine, *Revue Anglo-romaine,* that had its first number on December 1, 1895. Those who could not go behind the scenes could well hope that Leo XIII would soon recognize Anglican ordinations.

Chapter 7

Leo XIII (II)

There is every reason to believe that the chief author of *Apostolicae curae* was not, as has been said, Merry del Val, but the prefect of the Holy Office, former professor of dogmatics at the Collegio Romano, Cardinal Mazzella. The first draft of the letter, composed in Italian, is in his handwriting. A second draft, in Latin, was made in the course of the discussion of the Mazzella text by the members of the Holy Office. It remains close to Mazzella's Italian draft, which it expands at several places. The final text of *Apostolicae curae* bears numerous but slight modifications and additions. As appears from the documents in the Vatican Archives, many of these come from Leo himself, who penned them in.

As it is formulated in *Apostolicae curae,* Leo XIII's final judgment on the validity of Anglican orders is based on two central points, relating to "form" and to "intention." From these the pope infers that the Anglican Ordinal suffers from a fundamental deficiency, that he calls its "native character and spirit." We will limit our examination of the apostolic letter to these three items. Other details about Leo's document may be found in the abundant literature that is now available.

The Question of Form

The first question refers to "form." The pope's conclusion is that the Edwardine Ordinal of 1552, that contains the rite

according to which Matthew Parker was consecrated archbishop of Canterbury, is defective in regard to the form of the
sacrament of Orders. Sacramental hylomorphism is in fact
adequately elucidated in *Apostolicae curae:*

> In the rite for the performance and administration of any
> sacrament a distinction is justly made between its 'cere-
> monial' and its 'essential' part, the latter being now usually
> called its 'matter and form.' Moreover it is well known that
> the sacraments of the New Law, being sensible signs which
> cause invisible grace, must both signify the grace which they
> cause and cause the grace which they signify. Now this
> essential rite as a whole, that is, in both matter and form
> together, belongs chiefly to the form; for the matter is by
> itself the indeterminate part, which becomes determinate
> through the form.[1]

There was no problem with the matter: this was the laying
on of hands by the consecrators. But, in the hylomorphic
theory, matter has no effect without a form. The form for the
ordination of a presbyter according to the Ordinal was identified as "Receive the Holy Ghost . . . etc. . . ." Leo XIII concluded first that this form was defective, for it does not express
"the order of priesthood or its grace and power, which is
pre-eminently the power 'to consecrate and offer the true body
and blood of the Lord,' in that sacrifice which is no 'mere
commemoration of the sacrifice performed on the Cross.'"[2] In
other words, the form of ordination in the Ordinal does not
tally with the essence of the priesthood, which is connected
with the spiritual power to offer the Eucharist as the sacrifice
of Christ at Calvary made sacramentally present.

Passing on to the consecration of a bishop, Leo argued in
the same sense: the form, "Receive the Holy Ghost . . . etc . . ."
does not specify that episcopacy is "the high priesthood, the
sum total of the sacred ministry."[3] It therefore cannot confer
the episcopate any more than the previous form can confer the
priesthood.

The Question of Intention

The second major point of *Apostolicae curae* is treated more briefly: the ordination of Parker suffered also from a defect of "intention." In the Catholic tradition the basic principle for the effectiveness of a sacrament is that the minister must have the intention of "doing what the Church does." For when a human person who has been properly designated for this task administers a sacrament, this person acts in the name and for the sake of the Church. The Church, in this perspective, is the Church universal, also called the Church of Christ, the spiritual entity that, in the language of Vatican II, "subsists" on earth in visible structures that can be identified empirically as Churches.[4] When they are chosen to be ministers in such a visible structure in a local Church (that is, in the Catholic tradition, in a diocese), they become ministers in the Church universal. The intention to do what the Church does will normally be identical with what is said in the rites and formulae of the visible Church in which the minister functions. It follows that one ought not to oppose, though one may distinguish between, the ministers' subjective intention (what they have in mind), and the Church's intention as objectively formulated in the rites used by its ministers. In normal liturgical functions these two intentions coincide: the minister's subjective intention is at the service of the faithful in that it coincides with the Church's intention. Consequently, the question of intention is necessarily tied to that of form, the form being the rite that has been determined by the Church as the official expression of its intention. Since these rites and formulations have both a history and a contemporary context, the historical background is inseparable from the systematic explanation of intention at any given moment. Contemporary doctrine is always the outcome of a process of tradition.

Leo XIII thought that the consecrators of Parker did not intend to "do what the Church does" in ordination.[5] He inferred this defect of intention from his previous determination regarding defect of form. The consecrators showed their lack of the right intention when they selected a rite that had been altered for the manifest purpose of not doing what the Church does.

The fact that no other rite was legal in England in 1559 does not seem to have been considered. But what is the local Church to do, when totalitarian political authorities restrict the options?[6]

Pope Leo's Approach

Apostolicae curae concludes to defect of intention from defect of form, and to defect of form in the consecration of a bishop from defect of form in the ordination of a priest. This convoluted reasoning is largely responsible for the widespread confusion that is found in the commentaries on pope Leo's decision, whether these are favorable or hostile to his conclusion. Why did Leo choose this approach? There seem to be several reasons.

The first derives from the pope's basic method, namely, the neo-scholastic way of doing theology, that he had chosen as the standard for Catholic schools. Leo looked for clues in the sacramental theology of Thomas Aquinas. Precisely, the problem of what happens when the form of a sacrament is altered had been faced in *Summa theologica,* III, 9. 60, a. 8: *Utrum aliquid liceat addere verbis in quibus consistit forma sacramentorum?* In this part of the *Summa* St. Thomas answers the question of changing the rite of a sacrament by addition or subtraction, as priests are occasionally tempted to do. He successively examines the intention of those who introduce or use an altered form, and the sense of the altered formulation itself. In regard to intention:

> First, on the part of the one who says the words, whose intention is required for the sacrament . . . if by this addition or subtraction he intends to introduce a new rite that is not received by the Church, he does not seem to be effecting the sacrament, since he does not seem to intend to do what the Church does.[7]

If the rite is altered in order not to do what the Church does, it become invalid and the sacrament is not given.

This is confirmed by considering the sense of the alteration.

Thomas distinguishes between a minor and a major change. A minor change, as when a priest omits the word, *enim,* in *Hoc est enim corpus meum,* does not affect the sense of what is said. A major change, however, takes away the sense of the words. This happens, for instance, if baptism is given in the name of two Persons only, or in the name of the Virgin Mary! In such a case there is no sacrament.[8] For the formulation does not correspond to what the Church does in the sacrament.

In order to apply this to the case of the Ordinal of 1552, Leo XIII had two things to do. First, he had to investigate the intention of those who altered the rite of ordination, and then of those who used the new rite for the consecration of Matthew Parker. Second, he had to study the sense of the words in the rite of the Ordinal.

The Intention of the Framers of the Ordinal

The second reason for the mode of argumentation of *Apostolicae curae* derives from problems that emerged in these investigations. The chief author of the two Prayer Books of 1549 and 1552, and of the Ordinals of 1550 and 1552, was, as we have seen, especially concerned about the true doctrine of the eucharist. The basic purpose behind the Ordinal was therefore not hard to discover. Being thoroughly Zwinglian in sacramental theology, Thomas Cranmer wanted to erase from the liturgical books all endorsements of, or allusions to, the doctrines of the real presence and of transubstantiation, along with all suggestions that the eucharistic service—the mass—is somehow a sacrifice propitiatory. Yet special difficulties in the papal analysis of the Ordinal arose from the hylomorphic theology of the "matter and form" of a sacrament that was prevalent in neo-scholasticism.

There were in fact two different questions here. On the one hand, it had to be determined whether the altered form of the sacrament of Orders truly expressed Cranmer's Zwinglian intention to do away with the traditional conception of sacraments. On the other hand, one had to determine whether the new Ordinal could not, in spite of its author's intention, still convey the traditional sense of ordination. This question was not new: Cranmer himself had confronted it. It was because the bishop of Winchester, Stephen Gardiner, had read the doctrine of transubstantiation in the Prayer Book of 1549 that the Black Rubric was inserted in that of 1552.

No one questions the fact that Cranmer wanted to uproot the medieval conception that tied priesthood to a power over the confection of the sacrament. The scholastics, and, with them, Leo XIII, defined the priesthood by the "spiritual power" conferred to the priest, and the episcopate by the power conferred to the bishop. The priest's power was operative in regard to the sacramental body of Christ, which is the eucharist, and the bishop's power in regard to the mystical body, which is the Church.[9] In other words, in the hylomorphic sacramentalism that was operative in the theology of Leo XIII, the form of the sacrament of Orders had to express the spiritual power that pertains to priesthood and to episcopacy. Furthermore, as is made clear in *Apostolicae curae,* this power is, in the priesthood, essentially related to the offering of the eucharist: it is the power to offer the eucharistic sacrifice.

The Liturgical Data

At this point, Leo XIII ran into an additional difficulty. For the reference to this dimension of the eucharist has never been central to Western liturgies of ordination. The Pontifical of Leo XIII was that which had been promulgated by Clement VIII in 1596 and Urban VIII in 1644, and which was only slightly modified from the Roman Pontifical in use at the end of the Middle Ages. In the ordination of a priest there are two impositions of hands. The first, which is made by both the bishop and the priests who are present, takes place in silence, but the right hand remains extended during the long preface that follows. After the porrection of the instruments, the bishop imposes hands a second time, while he says: "*Accipe Spiritum Sanctum* . . . Whose sins you shall remit, they are remitted; whose sins you shall retain, they are retained." In the consecration of a bishop, there is a laying on of hands after the great prostration, while the consecrator says, "*Accipe Spiritum Sanctum*"; and this is also followed by a long preface. It is this preface that is commonly identified as the form of the episcopal consecration.[10]

In the actual words of the Pontifical, however, the sacrificial nature of the eucharist and the priesthood is not stressed at all. The tasks of a bishop are briefly listed: ". . . to judge, to interpret, to consecrate, to ordain, to offer, to baptize and to confirm." To "offer" is of course a much vaguer expression than "to offer a sacrifice propitiatory."[11] Moreover, the preface that follows the imposition of hands makes no mention of the eucharist. In the ordination of a priest the reference to the eucharistic sacrifice is slightly more stressed. "It belongs to a priest to offer, to bless, to govern, to preach, and to baptize." God is asked to bestow on him "the virtue [power] of sacerdotal grace" *(gratia sacerdotalis virtutis)*. But the preface says nothing of the eucharist. It is in the porrection of the instruments that the reference to the sacrificial priesthood is the clearest, when the bishop says: "Receive power to offer sacrifice to God and to celebrate mass for the living as well as for the dead." After the creed there is a second imposition of hands, when the bishop says, "*Accipe Spiritum Sanctum.* Whose sins you shall remit they are remitted; whose you shall retain they are retained." One may well understand why the porrection of the instruments, with the accompanying declaration, was considered by Thomas Aquinas to pertain to the matter and form of the sacrament of orders: this is the only place that has a clear reference to the eucharistic sacrifice.

The situation was much the same in all the medieval Pontificals, with the difference that, in several of them, the laying on of hands continued through the preface. The Pontificals that were in use in England before Henry VIII's *Act for the Consecration of a Bishop,* of 1542, had been influenced by the older Pontifical of Egbert (8th c.). They were related to that of the abbey of Bec in Normandy (12th-13th c.). They are believed to result from a conflation of Gallican and Anglican rubrics (in the geographic sense of these terms) with an older Roman type. The most commonly used, which became the only one in 1542, was the Sarum rite. This is the one that was altered in the composition of the Ordinals of 1550 and 1552.

The accent of the Sarum rite is placed on leadership and holiness. It is not more explicit than the Roman Pontifical as to the essence of the priesthood. Yet it also exhibits a special concern for doctrine. A public interrogation of the candidate to the episcopate takes place before the consecration, though not necessarily on the same day. The future bishop is required to make an explicit statement of belief in transubstantiation:

> Do you believe that the bread which is placed on the Lord's table is only bread before the consecration, but in that consecration, by the ineffable power of the Divinity, the nature and substance of that bread is changed into the nature and substance of the flesh of Christ, of no other flesh but that which was conceived of the Holy Spirit and born from the Virgin Mary? — I believe.[12]

There is a similar question for the wine.

Moreover, while the Sarum rite for the ordination of a priest gives the most prominent place to holiness, it also includes several mentions of the sacerdotal, cultic, sacrificial, or mystagogic aspect of the priesthood. To the general references to "offering" that are found in all Pontificals, Sarum adds several more passages, that relate chiefly to transubstantiation. In an optional exhortation to the candidates, the tasks shared by priests and bishops are said to be "catechizing, baptizing, celebrating mass, *changing the bread and wine into the body and blood of Christ,* preaching in church."[13] Priests and bishops are called "mediators between God and men . . ., [who] offer the prayers of the people to God by interceding for sinners." The porrection of the instruments is explained: "It pertains to them to confect the sacrament of the body and blood of Christ on the altar, to say prayers, and to bless the gifts of God."[14] The preface mentions that "the ministry of priests (*sacerdotum*)" is endowed with the spiritual means needed "for salutary offerings" (*ad hostias salutares*).[15] The vesting of the candidate ends on a prayer that includes another reference to transubstantiation: "Theirs be the task *to change* with undefiled blessing, for the service of Thy people, *the bread and wine into the body and blood of Thy Son.*"[16] Finally, an optional prayer before anointing the candidate's hands says: "Bless and sanctify, Lord, these hands of your priests for *consecrating offerings that are offered for the sins* and imperfections of Thy people . . ."

Clearly, the emphasis on transubstantiation and on offering the eucharist is much greater in the Sarum than in the Roman rite of ordination. This emphasis must have been introduced to offset the Berengarian theology of the eucharist, after Berengarius's condemnation in 1050 and his retraction in 1079.[17] But the authors of the Ordinal did not share the fear of over-spiritualizing the sacramental presence. Their elimination of all references to transubstantiation and to sacrifice propitiatory could be interpreted mildly, as a streamlining of a liturgy that had been overloaded with unnecessary theological theses, or rigidly, as a denial of basic Catholic doctrines. Pope Leo chose the rigid interpretation.

Pope Leo's Reasoning

These remarks throw light on Pope Leo's reasoning. In the Roman rite of the ordination of a bishop, the absence of allusion to the eucharistic sacrifice—theologically understood as specifying the essence of the sacerdotal function—is somewhat compensated by slight references to this sacrifice in the ordination of a priest. But in the Anglican Ordinal there is no such compensation. Whence the ordination of the latter is not identical with that of the former. In order to conclude further that the two rituals convey opposite conceptions of the sacramental priesthood, Leo had to repair to other documents of the English Reformation. Besides the writings of Cranmer and other churchmen and theologians, there were the Book of Common Prayer, the Homilies, and the Thirty-nine Articles. Article XXXI, read superficially, seemed to be conclusive:

> Wherefore the sacrifices of Masses, in which it was commonly said, that the Priest did offer Christ for the quick and the dead, to have remission of pain or guilt, were blasphemous fables, and dangerous deceits.[18]

The differences between the Ordinal and the Catholic rites were then taken by Leo XIII to result from a formal rejection of Catholic doctrines on the eucharist and the priesthood. This rejection in turn was attributed to a formal intention "not to do what the Church does" in ordination.

This interpretation of Article XXXI is not, however, self-evident. The plural formula, "sacrifices of masses," does sound strange to modern ears. Yet the expression was quite common in Catholic usage in the Middle Ages. But it did not designate the eucharistic sacrifice as such. It designated the eucharistic "sacrifice when used in the context of prayer for the dead as a sacrifice propitiatory." Such had been the formula of the profession of faith of Emperor Michael Paleologos, at the Second Council of Lyons in 1274: souls in purgatory can be assisted by "the sufrages of the living faithful, that is, the sacrifices of masses, prayers, almsgiving, and other acts of piety."[19] The formula, in fact, was not oriental, but Roman. The profession of faith had been previously proposed to the emperor by Pope Clement IV. The statement recurred, word for word, at the sixth session of the Council of Florence in 1439.[20] In other words, the phrase had a very special connotation. It pointed to the mass as a rite of propitiation applicable to the dead. It was a compromise—though heavy on the Roman side—between Eastern and Western conceptions of the intermediate state of the dead.

All the Reformers, however, saw this as a form of magic or superstition. To their ears it presented the eucharist as a pious work, by which one could acquire merit. And this was contrary to the principle of justification by faith. The rejection of "the sacrifices of Masses" in the Thirty-nine Articles was therefore not a denial that the eucharist could be called, in some sense, a sacrifice. It was a denial of more peripheral points of belief, namely purgatory and the efficacy of prayer for the dead.

Nativa indoles ac spiritus

What was finally determinative of Pope Leo's decision was not the Ordinal in its own choice of words, or the form of ordination in the Ordinal, or even the omission of previous ordination language. It was that all these points seemed to acquire an unfortunate doctrinal coloration from the theology of the English Reformers. Leo XIII was impressed by what he called the "native character and spirit of the Ordinal, as they say."[21] From this "native character" he inferred two points. First, the Ordinal, in its form of ordination, could not possibly convey the priesthood as traditionally understood. Second, it was inconceivable that, in the first years of the Elizabethan Reformation, and specifically at the consecration of Matthew Parker, those who used the Ordinal could have the proper intention to "do what the Church does."

What exactly is this *nativa indoles ac spiritus,* detected by Leo XIII? It would be a sort of natural drift of the Ordinal in a direction that would be ultimately incompatible with the Catholic understanding of orders and *sacerdotium,* and that would thereby make its use incompatible with the intention of doing what the Church does. It seems to be identical with what Francis Clark calls "the objective connotation of the whole Ordinal."[22] One arrives at it, Clark writes, "not merely by reference to Cranmer's heretical views, but by examining the actual wording and arrangement of the Ordinal, by comparing it with the Catholic Pontifical which it displaced, by interpreting it in the historical setting in which it appeared and was used, and by considering the unequivocal condemnation it received from the Catholic Church during the Marian restoration . . ." It is finally identical with the "intention of the Ordinal," which "not only fails to make sufficient those forms which are in themselves not duly determinate, but reduces to undue indeterminacy those forms which would normally be sufficient."[23] This "objective connotation" has "a bearing on both the defects on which Pope Leo pronounces."[24]

In other words, the "intention of the rite" is the key that reveals both a defect of form in the Ordinal and a defect of intention in the consecrator who uses the Ordinal. The *nativa indoles ac spiritus* is discovered by investigating the defect of form in the Ordinal; and the defect of form gains its negative effect from this *nativa indoles ac spiritus.* I fail to see how this type of reasoning escapes the vicious circle in which it is caught.

Moreover, we now know what escaped Leo XIII: there was no "unequivocal condemnation" of the Ordinal in the sixteenth century, except in the Recusants' polemical writings. The comparison of the Ordinal with the Pontifical did not convince Duchesne and De Augustinis of the former's invalidity. And

Cranmer's heretical views could well be considered irrelevant, in the light of the theological and canonical tradition that baptism given by heretics is valid and unrepeatable.

Conclusion

Rather than the recommendations of Duchesne and De Augustinis, solidly based on history and on theology, Leo XIII followed those of Pierotti and Mazzella, who read history in the light of neo-scholastic theology. This neo-scholastic theology was dear to Leo's heart. Yet this, I believe, was not determinative. The point that carried Pope Leo's option was the mirage of a flood of conversions. He was impressed by the rosy picture of the future that was painted by the English bishops: a condemnation of Anglican orders would unleash a steady stream of conversions. No doubt, the pope was the victim of wishful thinking. And this was not unrelated to the Roman triumphalism that was in part a sequel of earlier ultramontanism, in part a reaction against the loss of the Papal States.

It is ironic that Leo XIII was caught between two delusions. What had drawn him in the first place to study the question of Anglican ordinations was Portal's contagious conviction that the recognition of Anglican orders would not only change the unhealthy climate of relationships between Canterbury and Rome, but also tip the balance, within Anglican comprehensiveness, in favor of the Anglo-Catholic party. What finally persuaded Leo to choose the condemnation of Anglican orders was Cardinal Vaughn's mistaken hope that respect for the pope's judgment would bring the Anglo-Catholics into the Roman fold.

In formulating his decision, Leo XIII implicitly raised questions that were not foreseen by the Master of the Sacred Palace or by the members of the Holy Office. The main ones were brought up in the very moderate response that was made to his apostolic letter by the archbishops of Canterbury and York. *Apostolicae curae* assumed an interpretation of the English Reformation that was not shared by all historians. But should a papal decision be based on questionable historical presumptions? Theologically, Leo took as necessary to the transmission of orders a normative maximum regarding form and intention that was in fact missing in most of the liturgical tradition of the Catholic Church. In the matter of form, he demanded a uniformity that was contradicted by the history of ordinations in East and West. In the matter of intention, he looked for more than the intention to "do what the Church does." He required a detailed knowledge of, and assent to, doctrinal formulations of eucharistic doctrine that had never been clarified before the council of Trent, and a conception of prayer for the dead that was foreign to the Patristic theology of the eucharist.

One may well understand the archbishops' remark: "In overthrowing our orders, he overthrows all his own, and pronounces sentence on his own Church."[25]

Chapter 8

New Context

The pope's negative findings on Anglican ordinations did not provoke the promised influx of conversions. Some Roman Catholics in England, especially among the clergy, may well have found themselves vindicated and comforted by the papal decision. But its impact on Anglicans in general and Anglo-Catholics in particular was the opposite of what had been anticipated. A sense of injury and profound injustice among people, theologians, and clergy was the most tangible outcome of *Apostolicae curae* in the Church of England. Indeed, this could have been foreseen, had more Catholics been better attuned to the voices of Anglicanism than was the Roman Catholic hierarchy in the British Isles. One should at least have wondered if a negative conclusion would not open a sort of parallel to the Galileo case! But the forces that could not prevail in Rome in 1896 weighted on the reception of Leo's decision. The sharp edge of his condemnation was blunted by glitches in the process of reception. Furthermore, this was happening just at the time when the Church of England, branching out into many parts of the world as the Anglican Communion, was acquiring an ecumenical dimension that rendered obsolete the defensive nationalism of the reigns of Henry VIII, Edward VI, and Elizabeth.

Response of the Archbishops

We need not enter into details concerning the *Response of*

the Archbishops of England to the Apostolic Letter of Pope
Leo XIII on Anglican Ordinations, that was released at
Lambeth Palace in February, 1897.[1] Yet theological courtesy
requires that those who pay religious attention to the words of
the bishop of Rome should at least listen with an open mind
to the archbishops whom Leo's apostolic letter, if its conclusion
was correct, reduced, as it were, to the lay state. The response
was actually the work of the bishop of Salisbury, John Words-
worth, who had previously been in dialogue with Swedish
Lutherans and Old Catholics about episcopal succession in the
Anglican Communion. It was signed by the archbishops of
Canterbury and York, E.W. Benson and W.D. McLagan. The
tone is remarkably moderate. The Roman Church is called "a
sister Church of Christ" (n. II), and Leo XIII "our most vener-
able brother" (IV), "our brother" (XX).

The response reviews the evidence relating to the sacrament
of orders and the consecration to the episcopate (I-IV), to the
practice of Rome and of the papal legate in the sixteenth
century (VI), to the Gordon case (VII). The archbishops praise
Leo XIII for not resting satisfied with the "weak conclusions"
that could be drawn from such evidence, and for starting a
fresh investigation. But they regret that this has been done "in
appearance rather than in reality" (VIII). The archbishops
agree with the council of Trent's identification of the matter
and form of ordination. But, as they remark, the form was not
"defined either in the Word of God or by the Catholic Fathers
or Councils" (VIII).

After a digression on the form or forms of confirmation
(IX-X), the archbishops question the pope's method. It is, they
think, anachronistic: Leo argues from the council of Trent to
determine what should have been the form of the sacrament in
the Ordinal composed before that council. It also upsets the
traditional balance of doctrine and liturgy: at the pope's hands,
lex credendi has gone far beyond the confines of *lex orandi,* as
this stood in the Catholic tradition before the Reformation
(XI). The response has no difficulty showing that the old
tradition did not demand explicit statements on the sacrificial
dimension of the eucharist (XII) or the use of such grandilo-
quent episcopal titles as "high priest" or "pontiff" (XIII).

The archbishops discuss at length the pope's objections to

the form of the Ordinal (XIV-XVI). They note that his description of the Anglican intention ignores the clear statements of the preface (XVII). They explain and defend the removal of superfluous ceremonies, such as the porrection of instruments and anointing with chrism (XVIII). They hold that the powers given to the bishop at his consecration need not be formulated expressly. And they adduce a great deal of evidence to the effect that these powers "can be conveyed either implicitly and by usage, as was the method in ancient times, or at once and explicitly; but the method of conveyance has no relation to the efficacy of ordination."[2] They solemnly express the faith and intention of the Church of England:

> We therefore, taking our stand on Holy Scripture, make reply that in the ordering of Priests we duly lay down and set forth the stewardship and ministry of the word and Sacraments, the power of remitting and retaining sins, and other functions of the pastoral office, and that in these we do sum up and rehearse all other functions (XIX).[3]

Finally, the archbishops express their fear that the pope has implicitly condemned, along with Anglican orders, the orders of the Orthodox Church and of his own Catholic Church. They end, however, on an acerb note that is out of tune with the rest of the response, and is hardly helpful to their argumentation. While they recognise that the messages of Leo XIII on other questions "are sometimes very true and always written with a good will," they add: "But that error which is inveterate in the Roman communion, of substituting the visible head for the invisible Christ, will rob his good words of any fruit of peace" (XX).[4]

The archbishops' response was addressed to "the whole Body of Bishops of the Catholic Church." The Roman Catholic bishops of England and Wales took occasion of this to issue their rebuke. This document was entitled, *A Vindication of the Bull 'Apostolicae Curae',* 1897.[5] There is nothing new in it, as it repeats and develops what it takes to be the central argument of the bull, namely, the necessary ties between the true doctrine of the eucharistic presence and the validity of ordination to the priesthood. It underlines the lack of precision of the form used in the Ordinal. The letter maintains that the minister's intention is to be determined, not by later reinterpretations, but by the form of the rite, which itself expresses the intention of those who composed it. And it invites the archbishops to state clearly their belief in the "real objective" presence of Christ in the eucharist.

The archbishops did respond, in a letter to Cardinal Vaughn of March 12, 1898. They complained that, by centering the discussion on belief in the real presence, the letter of the English bishops was changing the parameters of the debate. As to them, they did not think that the medieval doctrine of transubstantiation was relevant to the validity of ordinations.

It should be obvious that this kind of tit for tat discussion leads nowhere. The debate at the level of the hierarchies should have ended with the archbishops' response. Yet the episode illustrates one aspect of the dilemma of Anglican orders. Arguments can be found for both sides. Yet the same event, interpreted several centuries later by Roman Catholic controversialists and by Anglican apologists, actually appears as two different facts. The historical event is lost behind a mist of theological a priori's that hide it at the very moment they interpret it. Thus have Catholics assumed that the *haeresis hujusmodi* of Julius III was the Anglican heresy, whereas it was only the marriage of priests. Likewise, Anglicans have maintained that the preface to the Ordinal is perfectly clear in formulating the intention of the Church of England regarding the continuity of orders since apostolic times; but Catholics who read the preface in the light of Cranmer's erroneous eucharistic conceptions found it too ambiguous to be taken at face value.

At this first level, the dilemma derives from the fact that diverse standards have been applied to the interpretation of the same historical texts.

The Question of Form

The first intimations that a new context for evaluating Anglican orders was in the making were delineated by the critique of *Apostolicae curae* that did not fail to be formulated in some Catholic circles. In fact, the reception of Leo's decision in Catholic theology has been marked by widespread confusion and disagreement as to the exact scope of the main points of the letter. Discussion has generally focused on three items: the historical survey that constitutes the first half of *Apostolicae curae,* the question of form, and the question of intention. There is no need for us to cover the historical survey again. For this would simply lead us back to the first chapters of the present review. Yet the questions of form and of intention have not lost their actuality.

Regarding form, it has not been difficult to show that the form of the sacrament of orders in the Catholic or the Orthodox Churches has not always explicitly mentioned the doctrine of the eucharist as a sacrifice, and that the form of the consecration of a bishop has not always called the bishop a "high priest." In fact, these two points have been made in the East more emphatically than in the West. The *Apostolic Constitutions* do connect ordination with the offering of *katharon anaimekton thusion* ("the pure and unbloody sacrifice . . ."),[6] while some later rituals, such as the Syrian Nestorian liturgy, refer only to "the episcopal ministry" in general terms. The Western liturgies are extremely sober.

The categories of matter and form, however, constitute a two-edged sword. In a book that he published shortly before *Apostolicae curae,* a French author, Abbé Gustave Delasges, argued that the ordination of Matthew Parker was certainly valid.[7] For the Ordinal preserved the proper matter and form, not indeed as they were elaborated in the Pontifical, but as they had been instituted essentially by Jesus Christ himself, namely, as laying on of hands with prayer. Yet the more recent argument of Anthony Stephenson against Anglican Orders was also based on the notion of matter and form: by virtue of the principle of *ex opere operato,* orders are validly conveyed only when the Catholic matter (laying on of hands) and form (the "preface" said by the ordaining bishop) are used.[8] Stephenson did not find the preface-form in the Ordinal. Ironically, this author joined the Anglican Church of Canada some years after writing his book; I presume he was no longer persuaded by his argument!

One has thus reached a second level of the dilemma. At this

level, the question concerns the essential form, or, if one prefers, the minimal form that is necessary and sufficient for ordination: were the medieval accretions that were left out in Cranmer's liturgical reform so necessary that their abandonment did invalidate the rite of the Ordinal?

The Question of Intention

Regarding intention, there has been a great deal of confusion as to the exact nature of the argumentation of *Apostolicae curae.* Some commentators have theorized that, in this document, defect of form is reduced to defect of intention, others that defect of intention is reduced to defect of form. Above all, there has been extensive debate on what Leo XIII meant by intention. Francis Clark has identified seven views:[9]

1. The intention in question is that of the "authors and framers" of the Ordinal.

2. It is the minister's *intentio circa significationem,* that is, his understanding of the meaning of the rite.

3. It is the "objective connotation of the whole Ordinal."

4. It is the minister's motive (position of Moyes, the member of Leo's Commission).

5. It is the "external intention of the minister, in the Catharinian sense." Ambrosius Catharinus, a distinguished but somewhat eccentric Dominican theologian in the sixteenth century, had his own theory: the minister's sacramental intention is not identical with his personal intention, but it is to be inferred from the meaning of the rite used.

6. It is the "intention of the Anglican Church" (the reading of *Apostolicae curae* by the two Anglican archbishops in their reply).

7. It is the "internal intention of the ordaining minister," not insofar as it is internal—of which "the Church does not judge" (a traditional canonical principle that is explicitly mentioned in *Apostolicae curae*)[10]—but insofar as it is expressed externally through the rite used. This is Clark's own reading of *Apostolicae curae.* Clark traces it back to the "principle of positive exclusion": Parker's consecrators had the intention, in keeping with the preface to the Ordinal, of making a bishop

according to the will of Christ, but they also excluded "an essential element of the sacrament of Order." This positive exclusion "nullified any general 'Christian' intention they may have had."[11]

I agree with Francis Clark that the ordaining bishop must personally have the intention to do what the Church does. However, I see no persuasive reason why the intention to do what the Church does would be nullified by the consecrator's erroneous theology of the eucharist and of orders. For, as was pointed out in 1896 by Gasparri and De Augustinis, "to do what the Church does" is not identical with "to intend what the Church intends."[12] One can intend what the Church does not intend, yet at the same time do what the Church does. Clark also thinks that the reasoning of *Apostolicae curae* is entirely adequate, and that, consequently it "needs no gloss or excuse: it remains wholly coherent and conclusive."[13] Whatever the inner coherence of *Apostolicae curae,* I am more sensitive to two points: *Apostolicae curae* is based in part on a mis-reading of Julius III and Paul IV; and the discrepancy is blatant between the momentous conclusion, that Anglican Orders "have been and are completely ineffective and totally null" (*irritas prorsus fuisse et esse, omninoque nullas*),[14] and the fact that the differences between the Roman and the Anglican rites of ordination, insofar as they explicitly refer to the sacerdotal or sacrificial nature of the Christian priesthood, remain minimal.

At this third level, the dilemma is compounded by a funda-mental question: why did not Leo XIII apply to ordination the decision of pope Stephen I on the efficacy of baptism given by heretics? Stephen's doctrine, formulated in 257,[15] outlawed the rebaptism of those who had been baptized in heresy, a practice that was common in North Africa and was defended by St. Cyprian. Admittedly, the Eastern Church, influenced by Firmilian of Caesarea's support of Cyprian, has never fully adjusted its theory or its practice on Stephen's doctrine. But, largely thanks to St. Augustine, the Western Church has uni-versally accepted Stephen's position on baptism. Scholastic theology generally extended it to all unrenewable sacraments, with the notable exceptions that have been mentioned in regard to medieval reordinations. Stephen's doctrine was the source of the theological principle that sacraments are valid *ex opere operato.* That is, they are made valid by what Christ, the High Priest, does, when the appropriate minister, in administering the sacrament, does what the Church does. The virtues, holiness, doctrines, or faith of the minister are irrelevant.

In the very scholasticism that Pope Leo praised so highly, this principle was central to sacramental theology. This remark uncovers an additional dimension of the Anglican orders dilemma. The debate on the Ordinal and Leo XIII's argumentation against the validity of its rite indicates that the extension of Stephen's doctrine to other sacraments than baptism was not taken for granted by Leo. In this case, however, a further question needs to be faced. Was Pope Leo, against so much evidence to the contrary, maintaining that Parker's consecrators had no intention to do what the Church does? Or was he excepting Parker's consecration from the general rule of sacramental efficacy *ex opere operato,* just as previous bishops had excepted simoniac ordinations? Or was he placing the fundamental question outside sacramental theology?

The Modes of Faith

Another point is related to the principle of *ex opere operato.* Since it is Christ himself who gives the sacrament through the Church's minister, it is proper to ask if the minister's intention to do what the Church does may not be expressed in different ways. The Catholic tradition has favored the doctrinal way: liturgy channels doctrine. *Lex credendi* and *lex orandi* are yoked together, the former being the inspiration for and the content of the latter. Yet liturgy does not only channel doctrine; it also channels divine grace. It is a credal formula, but also more than a statement of faith. As it favored doctrines and creeds, the Catholic tradition did not hesitate to expand the liturgical mode of expression, making it both verbal and non verbal. It includes rites and ceremonies that are visual no less than audial. This precisely illustrates the co-existence of many "modes" of faith. Faith exists and thrives in several modes, prosaic and poetic in its verbal forms, visual and audial in its instrumental organs, conscious and unconscious in its psychic level, cataphatic and apophatic in its affirmation, explicit and implicit, scientific and ordinary, theological and common. Undoubtedly one could discover many modes of faith, connected as these are with the many cultures of human civilization. In final analysis, each mode contributes to the wholeness of faith, as it relates faith to one or more dimensions within the wholeness of the believing human person.

This raises a point that is relevant to the discussion of Anglican orders. For if Thomas Cranmer did indeed espouse eucharistic doctrines that, seen in the light of the Catholic tradition, were heresies, it is also true that he was infinitely more skilled as a liturgist than as a theologian. Hence the question: did not his liturgy, by the traditional elements that it preserved from the Catholic past, convey the Church's faith on eucharist, priesthood, and orders, better than his theology did and intended? In other words, in order to judge whether the Ordinal serves as channel of the sacramental grace of orders, one has to focus attention on other modes of faith than the strictly doctrinal one. Such a concern was foreign to the neoscholastic mode advocated by Leo XIII. But one cannot afford to by-pass it in the contemporary ecumenical horizon.

The Cut-off Point of Apostolic Succession

The analysis of Paul IV's bulls that was made earlier in the present review may well provide an argument against Anglican ordinations. In explaining the documents of Julius III and Paul IV, I have insisted that the popes, especially Paul IV, did not wish to countenance in any way the rejection of papal primacy, the claims of royal supremacy, and the acts of the bishops who owed their entire promotion to the king (Edward VI) or the queen (Elizabeth). This decision was political no less than doctrinal. But the doctrine in question was not the affirmation of holy orders. It had to do with the then standard belief that episcopacy is not an order. If it is not an order, then the ritual of consecration need not signify the gift of sacramental grace, but only the granting of ordinary episcopal authority by the bishop of Rome and the gift of whatever actual grace (in medieval language, *gratia gratis data*) is necessary for the fulfilment of this function. When therefore the Recusants called "pseudobishops" those who were ordained according to the Ordinal, they saw an inseparable link between the signification of God's actual grace and that of the granting of jurisdiction by the bishop of Rome.

Two opposite lines of thought branch off from this point. On the one hand, considering the rite itself, one may wonder whether the link between the two aspects of the rite—the expression of doctrine and the expression of grace—is absolutely necessary. If it is not, then the sacramental grace may be communicated through a doctrinally deficient rite. On the other hand, it is difficult to escape another conclusion. Even though Parker was truly a bishop according to the rules of Paul IV, he himself could not, according to these rules, ordain or consecrate anyone with the Ordinal. In this case, the apostolic succession of bishops must have died, not indeed, as Leo XIII thought, at Parker's consecration, but in the consecrations that he himself performed. Such a conclusion is not based on the usual claim that the Ordinal is essentially invalid. But its conclusion is no less damaging for the historical transmission of apostolic succession in the Church of England and the Anglican Communion.

Not all these questions were brought to the surface in the months that followed 1896. Yet there was enough skepticism about Leo's apostolic letter, especially in France, to attract Leo's attention. On November 5, 1896, the pope addressed a letter to the archbishop of Paris, Cardinal François Marie Richard (1819-1908). The pope clearly affirmed that his intention in *Apostolicae curae* was to settle the matter once for all. He wanted to "judge absolutely and to decide definitely."[16] Moreover, he had done so "with such weighty arguments, with such clarity, and in so authoritative a manner, that no prudent man in good faith can revoke his sentence back into discussion, and that all Catholics must accept it with full obedience as being perpetually decided, firm, and irrevocable." It is on the basis of this letter that some Catholic circles have entertained the notion that the negative decision of *Apostolicae curae* was proclaimed infallibly.

Leo's apostolic letter, however, does not fulfill the conditions for infallibility that were itemized at Vatican Council I and reiterated at Vatican II: the bishop of Rome must be acting as "pastor and doctor of all Christians;" he must be defining a "doctrine belonging to faith or morals," to be held by the universal Church.[17] In order to defend the idea that *Apostolicae curae* contains an infallible decision, one has to fall back on the dubious belief that the bishop of Rome is also infallible concerning certain facts that would be necessary to the preservation of true doctrine. This notion was left out of the definition of infallibility at Vatican I. And it seems incompatible with the formula of Vatican II in *Lumen gentium:* "This infallibility with which the divine Redeemer wished to endow his Church in defining doctrine pertaining to faith and morals, is co-extensive with the deposit of Revelation . . ." (n. 25).

By no stretch of imagination can it be said that the condemnation of Anglican orders pertains to the deposit of divine Revelation, or that it is essential to the defense of the true faith concerning the eucharist, the priesthood, and the episcopate. In any case, Leo XIII himself excluded infallibility from *Apostolicae curae* when he called his decision "a point of discipline" (*caput disciplinae*).[18] Pope Leo's otherwise forceful formulation of his intention in issuing *Apostolicae curae* is in the same vein as those of Boniface VIII at the end of the bull *Unam sanctam* and of Pius V in the promulgation of the Tridentine form of the mass.[19] That is, it has authority until such a time as the Church may see fit to go another way.

Emergence of a New Context

Vatican Council II vaguely sketched the outline of a new horizon for relations between Canterbury and Rome when the decree on ecumenism, *Unitatis redintegratio,* selected the Anglican Communion for special mention among the "Churches and Ecclesial Communities of the West." At the Reformation, it said, "many communions, national or confessional, were separated from the Roman See. Among those in which Catholic traditions and institutions in part continue to exist, the Anglican communion occupies a special place."[20] There was no suggestion, however, as to what this place could be.

In another way too the council marked the emergence of a

new horizon for Anglican-Roman relations. For it took position against a principle that was operative in the theology of Thomas Aquinas and was basic to the very rules of Paul IV. This is the principle of the non-sacramentality of the episcopal consecration. The conciliar teaching on this point is embodied in the constitution *Lumen gentium:*

> The holy synod teaches that the fulness of the sacrament of orders is conferred by episcopal consecration, that fulness, namely, which both in the liturgical tradition of the Church and in the language of the Fathers of the Church is called the high priesthood, the acme of the sacred ministry . . . In fact, from tradition, which is expressed especially in the liturgical rites and the customs of both the Eastern and the Western Church, it is abundantly clear that by the imposition of hands and through the words of the consecration, the grace of the Holy Spirit is given, and a sacred character is impressed . . .

At this point, Vatican II departed from the scholastic theology of the episcopate, and aligned itself with what was already the Orthodox view. There may be different theories on the historical origin and development of episcopacy. On this matter the council did not take sides. Yet what is signified and given in the consecration of a bishop is no less than the grace of the sacrament of orders at the highest degree of this sacrament. For this reason, the liturgical reform that has followed Vatican II has preferred the phrase, "ordination of a bishop," to the term that was previously common, "consecration."

Reform of the Sacrament of Orders

In relation to the sixth sacrament, however, the emergence of a new context for the discussion of Anglican orders had begun before Vatican II, with Pope Pius XII's apostolic constitution *Sacramentum ordinis,* of November 30, 1947. Pius XII explicitly excluded the porrection of instruments from the matter of ordination. This ceremony, the pope stated, was not required "by the will of Our Lord Jesus Christ for the substance and validity of the sacrament."[21] Furthermore, "if it was at one time made necessary to [the sacrament's] value by the Church's will and statute, all know that the Church can change and abrogate its statutes." The pope determined that the matter of the sacrament is simply the laying on of hands.[22] For the priesthood, it is "the first laying on of hands, that is done in silence";[23] for episcopacy it is "the laying on of hands that is done by the consecrator." As for the form, it is, in both cases, contained in the "preface."

The logical conclusion was drawn by Paul VI in his reform of the sacrament of orders and its liturgy. In a series of *motu proprio* documents, Pope Paul reestablished the permanent diaconate (*Sacrum diaconatus ordinem,* June 18, 1967), reformed the Pontifical, bringing the ordination of bishops closer to the oriental tradition, doing away with the porrection of instruments in the ordination of a priest, and generally simplifying and clarifying the rite (*Pontificalis romani recognitio,* June 18, 1968). For the form of the three sacred orders he was more precise than Pius XII, in that he specified which are "the words of the consecratory prayer . . . that belong to the essential nature [of the sacrament] so that they are required for the validity of porter and exorcist and the subdiaconate (*Ministeria quaedam,* August 15, 1972).[24] Unlike Thomas Cranmer, however, he kept the orders of lector and acolyte. He finally established norms for the permanent diaconate and for admission of candidates to the priesthood (*Ad Pascendum,* same date).

The chief thrust of this reform was to render the ritual of ordination less disparate than it had been. Paul VI himself stated that he followed the principle of remaining closer to the early patristic rites and to those of the Oriental Church. By so doing, he also narrowed the gap between the Ordinal and the Pontifical.

"Sister Churches"

The new context acquired a clearer shape on October 25, 1970, when Paul VI canonized forty martyrs who had been victims of the English Reformation. Pope Paul selected this occasion, that was in itself inauspicious for Catholic-Anglican relations, to introduce a new perspective. Turning to the future, Paul VI declared:

> There will be no seeking to lessen the legitimate prestige and the worthy patrimony of piety and usage proper to the Anglican Church when the Roman Catholic Church—this humble 'Servant of the servants of God'—is able to embrace her ever beloved sister in the one authentic Communion of the family of Christ, a communion of origin and of faith, a communion of priesthood and of rule, a communion of the saints in the freedom of love of the Spirit of Jesus. Perhaps we shall have to go on waiting and watching in prayer in order to deserve that blessed day. But already we are strengthened in this hope by the heavenly friendship of the forty martyrs of England and Wales who are canonized today.[25]

Explicitly, Paul VI recognizes here that the Anglican Communion has the making of a Sister Church. Explicitly also, he promises that its "patrimony of piety and usage" will be respected whenever the two Communions are able to embrace each other as Sister Churches. Admittedly, one should not read too much in this expression. Pope Paul does not say that the two Communions are now Sister Churches. He says that they should be. He is proposing a model for their coming reconciliation. As I read this, however, it seems to me that Paul VI implicitly admits the value of the liturgy that is at the heart of the "piety and usage" of Anglicans. And this is the liturgy of the Book of Common Prayer, which includes the Ordinal.

The Ecclesiology of koinonia

Another step in the shaping of a new context was taken in January 1968. This was done by the Preparatory Commission that was set up between Paul VI and Archbishop Ramsey to prepare a direct official dialogue between the two Churches. The report of this Commission—usually called the Malta Report—includes the following passage:

We are agreed that among the conditions required for intercommunion are both a true sharing in faith and the mutual
recognition of ministry. The latter presents a particular difficulty in regard to Anglican Orders according to the traditional judgment of the Roman Church. We believe that the
present growing together of our two Communions and the
needs of the future require of us a very serious consideration
in the light of modern theology. The theology of the ministry
forms part of the theology of the Church and must be
considered as such. It is only when sufficient agreement has
been reached as to the nature of the priesthood and the
meaning to be attached in this context to the word 'validity'
that we could proceed, working always jointly, to the application of this doctrine to the Anglican ministry today. We
would wish to re-examine historical events and past documents only to the extent that they can throw light upon the
facts of the present situation.[26]

It is quite remarkable that this text locates the problem of
Anglican orders in ecclesiology rather than in sacramentology,
that is, in an area where it had not been placed by the Catholic
polemicists of the past. To what extent Pope Leo had seen the
problem in the light of ecclesiology is itself a matter of dispute,
since *Apostolicae curae* did not discuss ecclesiology.

In the dialogue that followed the creation of a Joint Commission, ARCIC-I did not discuss Anglican ordinations. Instead, it picked up the challenge from Malta at the point
where the Report envisaged a preliminary agreement on "the
nature of the priesthood." This was the topic of the Canterbury
Statement in 1973, *Ministry and Ordination,* that was itself
prepared by the Windsor Statement on *Eucharistic Doctrine,*
of 1971. The agreement on priesthood was completed, and
related to ecclesiology, in the Venice Statement of 1979, and
the Second Windsor Statement of 1981, on *Authority in the
Church,* I and II.

ARCIC-I went still further along the ecclesiological lines
recommended in the Malta Report. For its Final Report (1981)
drew attention to the underlying ecclesiology of its agreement.
This was an ecclesiology of Communion: "Fundamental to all
our statements is the concept of *koinonia* (communion)"

(n.4).[27] This concept was explained: "*Koinonia* with one another is entailed by our *koinonia* with God in Christ. This is the mystery of the Church" (n.5).[28] The Final Report further indicated that the agreed statements on *Eucharistic Doctrine* and on *Ministry and Ordination* presuppose a *communio*-ecclesiology. It was therefore by no means accidental that ARCIC-I inserted the following remark in the conclusion of the Canterbury Statement:

> We are fully aware of the issues raised by the judgment of the Roman Catholic Church on Anglican Orders. The development of the thinking in both our communions regarding the nature of the Church and of the ordained ministry, as represented in our Statement, has, we consider, put these issues in a new context (n. 17).[29]

This new context is no other than the consensus that has emerged in the dialogue between the two Communions. This perception is affirmed in the *Elucidations* of 1970: ARCIC-I

> believes that our agreement on the essentials of eucharistic faith with regard to the sacramental presence of Christ and the sacrificial dimension of the eucharist, and on the nature and purpose of priesthood, ordination, and apostolic succession, is the new context in which the questions should now be discussed. This calls for a reappraisal of the verdict on Anglican Orders of *Apostolicae curae* (n. 6).[30]

Cardinal Willebrands's Letter To ARCIC-II

Out of this new context there should arise a fresh way of looking at the question of Anglican orders. This is the gist of Cardinal Johannes Willebrands' letter addressed to the co-chairs of ARCIC-II on July 13, 1985. The letter sums up *Apostolicae curae*. The president of the Secretariat for the Unity of Christians sees the heart of Leo's apostolic letter in the perception of a *nativa indoles ac spiritus* in the Ordinal. The Ordinal, as Leo saw it, had been emptied of "all references to some of the principal axes of Catholic teaching concerning the relationships of the eucharist to the sacrifice of Christ and to the consequences of this for a true understanding of the nature of the Christian priesthood."[31] From this central idea, Pope Leo drew the conclusion that there were defects "both in the sacramental form and in the intention which the rite itself expressed."

Over against this, however, the "liturgical renewal" in both Communions, the bi-lateral dialogue and ARCIC-I's agreements have opened the way to the expectation that, at the end of its evaluation of the Final Report, the Anglican Communion will be able "to state formally that it professes the same faith concerning essential matters where doctrine admits no difference."[32] Then, "in the context of such a profession of faith, the text of the Ordinal might no longer retain that *nativa indoles* which was at the basis of Pope Leo's judgment."

Cardinal Willebrands' letter implies a rather different reading of *Apostolicae curae* than was made above. Yet this does not detract from the importance of the perspective that has been opened by the then president of the Council for Christian Unity. The full scope of this perspective emerges in the light of yet another insight of cardinal Willebrands regarding the possibility of many *typoi* of the Church within one Communion.

More on the Communio-*Ecclesiology*

Recent theological writings have taken the concept of Communion as the key to ecclesiology. It is increasingly recognized that the different aspects of the ecclesiology of Vatican II converge upon an ecclesiology of Communion that underlies all its statements.

The first major application of an ecclesiology of Communion to ecumenical problems and to the relations between Churches was made by Cardinal Willebrands himself. In an address given on January 18, 1970, in the church of Great St. Mary's in Cambridge, the cardinal elaborated on the fact the universal Church is made of local Churches. In so doing, he used a notion which, he said, "has received much fruitful attention from theologians recently."[33] These local Churches may well be patterned on different τυποι. The notion of type, "in the sense of general form or character," was explained in this way:

> Where there is a long coherent tradition, commanding men's love and loyalty, creating and sustaining a harmonious and organic whole of complementary elements, each of which supports and strengthens the other, you have the reality of a *typos.*
>
> Such complementary elements are many. A characteristic theological method and approach.... A spiritual and devotional tradition.... A characteristic canonical discipline, the fruit also of experience and psychology....
>
> Through the combination of all these, a *typos* can be specified.[34]

Now, this line of thought can be extremely fruitful in ecumenical theology. For the Churches of the West have developed along different lines since the Reformation, each of which has given shape to a specific ecclesial *typos*. But if there is an Anglican *typos* of the Church, then the criteria for evaluating Anglican orders ought to be taken from the characteristics of the Anglican *typos*, or, better said, from the universal Church as it is manifested in the Anglican *typos*. The characteristics of the Roman Catholic *typos* provide no adequate tool for judging the Anglican *typos*. Along this perspective, the new context is marked by the rise of a methodology of a more ecumenical scope than could be encompassed by the neo-scholasticism of Leo XIII.

In a *Communio*-ecclesiology, each Communion that is a part of the whole keeps its liturgical and doctrinal integrity. To what extent this integrity may allow for differences with another Communion should be a topic for discussion as the Churches attempt to restore their Communion along holistic lines.

Conclusion

It may be too early at this time to give a final judgment on how the *Communio*-ecclesiology may bring about a new view of Anglican ordinations in the Roman Catholic hierarchy. Yet there are signs that a change of perspective is not too much to expect in the foreseeable future. I will mention two such signs.

The first comes from a post-conciliar agency that has not, since its creation in 1969, been noted for its ecumenical concerns. In 1973, the International Theological Commission studied "the apostolicity of the Church and apostolic succession." The resulting document includes a section entitled, "Elements for an Evaluation of Non-Catholic Ministries." After speaking of the "Orthodox Church and the other churches which have retained the reality of apostolic succession," and before looking at "the communities issued from the sixteenth-century Reformation," the text turns to the Anglican Churches:

> Fruitful dialogues are taking place with Anglican communions (*sic*) which have retained the laying on of hands, the interpretation of which has varied. We cannot here anticipate the eventual results of this dialogue which seeks in what measure the factors that are constitutive of unity are included in the preservation of the rite of the laying on of hands and of the accompanying prayers.[35]

It is thus acknowledged that the Anglican Communion has preserved the traditional laying on of hands (the "matter"), along with "accompanying prayers," in which the Catholic tradition has commonly seen the "form" of the sacrament of orders. Only one difference with the Orthodox Church is noted. In Orthodoxy there is "unanimity concerning the unbroken coherence of scripture, tradition and sacrament." In Anglicanism, however, "the interpretation" [of the laying on of hands] has varied. If this is correct, then the International Theological Commission has suggested a way out of the dilemma inherited from Leo XIII. For it would then logically be enough, for Roman Catholic recognition of Anglican orders, to ascertain that the official, or standard, or more common, interpretation of orders is, within the Anglican ecclesial *typos*, in agreement with the Orthodox and Catholic interpretation.

The second sign comes from the evolving Roman attitude regarding Anglican bishops. On June 19, 1918, the secretary of State of Pope Benedict XV, Cardinal Gasparri (the same person who had studied Anglican orders at the time of Leo XIII), writing to the primates of the Lutheran Churches of Scandinavia, could not find a better title for them than, *perillustres viri,* "most famous men."[36] It is likely that, had there been a suitable occasion, Anglican bishops would have received a similar title! John XXIII opened the way to a different practice when, on December 2, 1960, he received Archbishop Geoffrey Fisher on a private visit of courtesy, the first such visit by an archbishop of Canterbury since the Reformation. After Vatican II and its ecumenical opening, Paul VI received Archbishop Michael Ramsey officially, and, on March 24, 1966, both of them led a prayer service in the church of St. Paul-outside-the-Walls. Anticipating this occasion, Pope Paul declared on March 20: "It is not yet a visit of perfect unity, but it is a visit of friendship placing [us] on the way to unity."[37] Michael Ramsey's successor in the see of Canterbury, Donald Coggan, also paid an official visit to Pope Paul VI, in April 1977. On April 28, the archbishop and Cardinal Willebrands presided at a ceremony for the blessing of new gates at St. Paul-outside-the-Walls. On April 29, the pope and the archbishop presided at a liturgy of the word in the Sistine chapel.

John Paul II has followed the example of Paul VI. In the course of his pastoral journey in England he was welcomed by Archbishop Robert Runcie at the cathedral of Canterbury on May 29, 1982. On the occasion of visits by Anglican bishops to the Vatican, Pope John Paul has invited them to bless the people with him: this is essentially a priestly action.

One may read such events as witnessing to a growing papal practice of treating the bishops of the Anglican Communion as true bishops. Given the evolving theological concern for the many aspects of Communion that have been preserved in spite of the separations of the past, the existential behavior of the modern popes in their face to face encounters with archbishops of Canterbury acquires an ecclesiological dimension. It underlines the increasing obsolescence of the rules that were determined by Leo XIII in other circumstances.

Conclusion

The Solution

It is my impression that, outside the British Isles and Ireland, the Roman Catholic laity who have had dealings with Anglicans take it for granted that their ministers are priests in the Catholic sense of the word: the contention that Anglican orders are invalid in the absolute (ontological) sense has not generally passed into the *sensus fidelium*. Whether this is to be attributed to ignorance of papal legislation, or to a deeper spiritual sensitivity than is shared by the hierarchy, is a moot point that need not be decided.

It also seems undeniable that Catholic theologians who have been engaged in ecumenical dialogue with members of the Anglican Communion are now considerably embarrassed by Leo XIII's negative findings. The condemnation of Anglican orders as absolutely invalid has had the opposite effect to what Pope Leo and the English Catholic hierarchy expected. At the time of unionism, one could entertain the hope, however unrealistic, that reunion would come about if a high number of Anglicans discovered the nullity of their orders and sacraments. At the time of ecumenism, however, a perspective of this sort makes no sense. The negative position of Leo XIII has become counterproductive, making ecumenical relations between the Communions much more delicate than they ought to be. It is no exaggeration to say that the recognition of Anglican orders by the Catholic hierarchy has now become imperative. The question is whether and how this can be done gracefully. In these conditions, it is urgent to ask how the Church can in the future escape the impasse of *Apostolicae curae*.

What is sacramental validity?

The first point to ascertain is the exact scope of the notion that sacraments are valid or invalid. Since the Church does not judge what is purely interior to the conscience, the magisterium can never assert that divine grace, sanctifying, sacramental, or actual, has not been received. What it can say, and has said, is that in certain circumstances, the sacrament that has allegedly been given cannot be recognized as a sacrament. Paul IV could not recognize a consecration to the episcopate that explicitly denied the prerogatives of the bishop of Rome among the Church's bishops. Leo XIII could not recognize the externals of the sacrament of orders in ordinations and consecrations done according to the Ordinal. In neither case does this imply that the sixth sacrament was never in fact given, or sacramental grace and character received, through the Ordinal. It only implies what it says: the sixth sacrament, even if present and effective, could not be recognized. For the members of the Catholic Church who are aware of this non-recognition, however, there naturally follows a presumption of ineffectiveness in the Anglican ordinations, on the basis of the extrinsic probability that the popes involved were not mistaken. But one cannot say more than that. The conclusion that Paul IV's or Leo XIII's decisions directly affected the existence of the sacrament of orders in the Church of England cannot be drawn from its non-recognition by these Roman pontiffs. Invalidity today can mean no more than what it meant before the theologians of the Counter Reformation came to think that they had access to the essence of reality. It simply means non-recognition of the externals of the sacrament of orders. As Bishop Christopher Butler summed it up in 1967 for the Preparatory Commission, the Roman Catholic Communion "does not acknowledge the validity—but does not contest the efficacy—of Anglican ordained ministry."[1]

Parameters of the Problem

The second point is to define the exact parameters of the

remaining problem. In principle, there is no difficulty to consider that the only papal statement that need to be assessed today is that of Leo XIII. Although most of the present review has dealt with the more remote history of the matter, and Pope Leo himself argued from historical precedent, the contemporary issue does not concern Matthew Parker's consecration in 1559. It deals with the question whether and how the disciplinary decision formulated in *Apostolicae curae* can, or should, be reversed, by-passed, or ignored.

There are clear limits to what can be reasonably expected from the Catholic Church in this matter. I am personally convinced that Leo XIII's reasoning was flawed by several historical mistakes, and by theological presuppositions that were inadequate, yet hardly avoidable in the neo-scholasticism of the late nineteenth century. This does not make the pope's decision false. The category of truth or untruth does not apply to disciplinary decisions. These come under other categories of a more pragmatic sort. They are justified or unjustified, proper or improper, applicable or inapplicable, up to date or obsolete, relevant or irrelevant to the situation. And there may be innumerable shades and nuances between these alternatives. In the history of the older papacy (before the Counter Reformation), popes were not reluctant to undo what had been done, or reject what had been said, by their predecessors. Besides the cases of Liberius (pope, 352-366), Vigil (pope, 537-555), and Honorius (pope, 625-638) in patristic times,[2] those of Formosus and John XXII (pope, 1316-1334)[3] can illustrate the point. In the more recent papacy, there would seem to be no difficulty for a pope to criticize another who is several century distant in time (as Boniface VIII was from Pius XII).[4] Yet it may be more delicate for a pope in our century to contradict Leo XIII, who lived barely one hundred years ago. The art of reaching theological conclusions should not spurn the diplomatic art of ecclesiastical face-saving.

Several Solutions
The third point, therefore, consists in searching for a solution

of the question of Anglican orders that would have a door open for those who hold that Leo XIII was, after all, right. Several solutions, that need not be mutually exclusive, have in fact been proposed.

(1) Presumption of Validity

The Catholic hierarchy could decide that there is, today, if not in the past, a presumption of validity in favor of Anglican orders.[5] From Paul IV to Leo XIII there was a presumption of invalidity. The circumstances having been drastically altered, this presumption of invalidity need not apply any longer. Arguments in support of a presumption of validity may be drawn from several areas: the general predominance, in contemporary Anglicanism, of "high church" over "low church" conceptions of the sacraments; the present evidence that Anglican bishops intend to do what the Church does in ordination; the participation of Old Catholic bishops in Anglican ordinations;[6] the growth of a theology of priesthood that is shared by Catholics and Anglicans alike, as illustrated by the Final Report; the increasing mistrust of the Aristotelian categories of form and matter in sacramental theology; the progressive abandonment of a "pipe-line" conception of apostolic succession in Catholic theology; the recognition of Anglican orders by Orthodox Churches by virtue of the "principle of economy."[7]

In a first step, this would allow Catholic bishops to ordain conditionally, rather than absolutely, those Anglican or former Anglican priests and deacons who ask for it. In a second step, it could allow the Catholic magisterium to declare that, given the contemporary evidence in favor of the presumption of validity, Anglican orders are now recognized, or regarded as valid.

(2) Implications of Ecclesial Status

The Catholic Church could abandon altogether its previous search for validity in the Anglican ritual for ordination. For what is ultimately the ordaining agent is the ecclesial Communion, of which the bishop acts as the representative. Since it is only in the horizon of ecclesial Communion that a bishop can act as the transmitter of orders in apostolic succession, the decisive point in the transmission of orders is not the ritual as such, but the ecclesial context in which the ritual is agreed upon and used.[8] It is this context that provides a liturgical action with its effective symbolism. A sacrament may be given even with a deficient ritual, because *Ecclesia supplet,* the Church supplies for what may be missing, defective, or imperfect in the acts and words of the minister. In this case, the recognition that the Anglican Communion is indeed a Sister Church would imply the validity of its orders. Where there is sufficient evidence that a religious community is a Church in the Catholic sense of the term, then it is obvious that such a community has proper orders and ministry.

This would be in line with the growing feeling that the right setting for the solution of the question of Anglican orders is not sacramentology, but ecclesiology. One may express this in the words of the regional dialogue between Anglicans and Roman Catholics in California:

> Our understanding is that the critical questions are: is there Church here? Is there ministry here? . . . In each community the president of the eucharistic assembly is ordained and the authority to minister comes from Christ through bishops designated to confer authority. We recognize in each other fidelity to the tradition of the apostolic church. This leads us to ask the question: do Anglican priests and Roman Catholic priests do essentially the same thing when they celebrate the eucharist?[9]

In this problematic, it is the recognition of ecclesial status that leads to recognition of orders and eucharist.

(3) *Ecclesia Supplet*

A way to recognize Anglican orders without passing judgment on *Apostolicae curae* may be adapted from traditional sacramental theology and the discipline of the sacraments. It is generally admitted that *Ecclesia supplet,* the Church corrects whatever incorrections have been unintentionally introduced in the performance of a sacrament. And one can argue that, even in spite of Cranmer's intention in composing and imposing the Ordinal, in spite of the personal theology of some, possibly many, among the Edwardine and Elizabethan bishops, the Church of England as a whole intended to do what the Church does without doctoring this intent with their eccentric theologies. In this vein, Jean-Marie Tillard has thought that Protestant orders could be validated by virtue of the principle, *Ecclesia supplet,* on the basis of the implicit desire for the eucharist that is present in authentic baptism, the three sacraments of Christian initiation—baptism, confirmation, euchar- ist—being theologically inseparable.[10]

On such a basis, and in light of the new ecumenical horizon, the bishop of Rome could solve the question by extending to Anglican ordinations a practice that is occasionally used as a means to validate an invalid marriage: *sanatio in radice* (canons 1161-1165 in the code of 1983). Such an extension would be analogical; and the analogy is admittedly not perfect, since there is no parity between the two sacraments of matrimony and of orders. A *sanatio in radice* is possible when the ministers of matrimony, who are, in Catholic theology, the spouses themselves, are living and are by their life expressing consent to their marriage. In the strict sense, a *sanatio* of ordination *in radice* could be done only when the ordainers are still living and have kept their intention to do what the Church does. It could not work if the ordainers are no longer living. And it could not be retroactive into past centuries. But the urgent problem is not for the past; it is for the present and the future.

(4) A Suggestion From the Lutheran/Catholic Dialogue

A recommendation that was made in 1970 by "Lutherans and Roman Catholics in Dialogue" in the USA, may be in-

voked in favor of Anglican orders. The Catholic members of
this official American dialogue made the following statement:

> As Roman Catholic theologians, we acknowledge in the
> spirit of Vatican II that the Lutheran communities with
> which we have been in dialogue are truly Christian churches,
> possessing the elements of holiness and truth that mark
> them as organs of grace and salvation. Furthermore, in our
> study we have found serious defects in the arguments cus-
> tomarily used against the validity of the eucharistic Ministry
> of the Lutheran churches. In fact, we see no persuasive
> reason to deny the possiblity of the Roman Catholic Church
> recognizing the validity of this Ministry. Accordingly we
> ask the authorities of the Roman Catholic church whether
> the ecumenical urgency flowing from Christ's will for unity
> may not dictate that the Roman Catholic church recognize
> the validity of the Lutheran Ministry and, correspondingly,
> the presence of the body and blood of Christ in the eucha-
> ristic celebrations of the Lutheran churches.[11]

This recommendation was justified by a broader notion of
apostolic succession than that which is restricted to the succession of bishops, by the historical evidence of ordinations by
medieval abbots who were not bishops, and by the assumption
that the Church has received from Christ, and can use in the
power of the Holy Spirit, extensive authority over the sacraments and the forms of their administration.[12] There are admittedly reasons that militate against the relevance of this recommendation in the matter of Anglican orders. First, the dia-
logants themselves did not wish to make their recommendation
a general principle applicable to other ecclesial and theological
situations than those of Lutheran Churches: "We do not wish
our statement concerning Lutherans to be thought to be applicable to others without further and careful consideration . . ."[13]
Second, Lutheran orders are not claimed to be given by
bishops: even though the Lutheran bishops of Scandinavia are
in uninterrupted succession with their Catholic predecessors,

ordination by bishops is not considered as being dogmatically necessary. Third, a recommendation by theologians has no authority by itself; it needs to be received by the Church at large and to be endorsed by the magisterium, a process that has so far not taken place.

Nonetheless, the recommendation deserves consideration: if an eventual recognition of Lutheran orders is at all conceivable in Catholic theology, all the more so a recognition of Anglican orders.

(5) Supplemental Regularization

By this awkward expression I designate the suggestion, that is widely accepted in the Protestant world, that some mutual regularization of orders and ministries is appropriate when two Churches decide to become one. That this may be applicable to the differences between Roman Catholics and Anglicans regarding the value of the Ordinal was suggested by Bishop Christopher Butler in the discussions that led to the Malta Report of 1968. As he remarked, the Anglican bishops who were gathered at the Lambeth Conference of 1920 declared their readiness "in the interests of the achievement of full communion, to consider such 'regularization' of the Anglican ministry as might be required by the party with which unity was to be attained."[14] Should the present or future Anglican bishops share this readiness, then an agreement could be negotiated regarding what supplemental regularization may be needed before the Catholic Church is willing and able officially to recognize Anglican orders. Although I do not favor this solution,[15] I must acknowledge that the suggestion has been seriously made and is worth considering. It would help overcome the scruples of many Roman Catholics who are rightly, though perhaps overly, concerned about the integrity of the sacrament of orders. It would at the same time bring the Roman Catholic-Anglican dialogue closer to the pattern that was recommended by the Faith and Order Commission in the "Lima Report" on *Baptism, Ministry, Eucharist* of 1982 (the "BEM").[16]

The Problem of Jurisdiction

The notion of sacramental validity is related to the difficult theological question of the nature of jurisdiction. This notion was transferred from civil law to canon law in the course of the codification of church laws, in the first half of the Middle Ages. But theological reflection has been unable to determine what the nature of jurisdiction can be. Before the fourteenth century, jurisdiction was not located in the powers of the bishop or priest but in the "subjects" of their authority. A bishop without subjects (for instance, a retired or deposed bishop) could do nothing authoritatively, his power being like a "form" without its "matter." Thus, ordinations done by someone in the position of Archbishop Lefebvre would be null. In the fourteenth century, however, during the controversy over papal authority that was sparked by the Great Western Schism, jurisdiction came to be conceived as a power inherent in the bishop or priest. In 1974, I concluded from this that "there is no proper analogy between the reordination of priests previously ordained by a simoniac bishop, and that of Protestant or Anglican ministers."[17] For the first was done with the older notion of jurisdiction in mind, and the second with the newer notion.

At the present time, however, I do not think that this reasoning is correct. For if the second view may well have been predominant in the sixteenth century, the older view remained operative for a long time. I think that it was at work in the decisions of Paul IV as he treated the Ordinal-consecrated bishops as without jurisdiction. In fact, it was still the basis on which the Recusant, Matthew Kellison, in 1629, understood the difference between a priest and a bishop. Bishops, Kellison explains, receive both a power of order and a power of jurisdiction, either from Christ at their consecration, or from the pope (or the Church) in the bull that confirms their election: the two theories "are probable."[18] However, one may ask the partisans of the first theory how they explain the difference between bishops, who can ordain, confirm, etc., and priests, who cannot . Kellison writes:

> To this they answer, that although all Bishops and Priests receive their Jurisdiction in respect of the active power which

> it implyeth, immediatlie from Christe in their ordination,
> yet they cannot exercise it, unless by the Pope subjects be
> given them and applyed to them, as they are to the Bishop
> in his Diocese, and to the Pastour in his Parish, and not out
> of it . . . For (sayeth Dominicus Sotus) as, although a man
> have a key fit and apte of it selfe to open a locke, yet it
> cannot open it unlesse it be applyed. So although a Bishop
> or Priest have the Key of Jurisdiction; yet he cannot exercise
> it but on them who are applyed as subjects unto him.[19]

Thus it is the absence of subjects that prevents some bishops
or priests from exercising their orders; and subjects, Kellison
says, are given them by the pope.

The Council of Trent did the best it could in the circumstances. It did not opt for a theory of jurisdiction. Nor did it
say that Protestant or Anglican ministers receive no power of
orders. Rather, it said that "those who have been neither properly ordained nor sent (*rite ordinati nec missi*) by ecclesiastical
and canonical power, but come from elsewhere, are not legitimate ministers of word and sacraments."[20] Illegitimacy, however, need not imply more than illiceity.

By the time of Leo XIII, the first conception of jurisdiction
was forgotten. The nuances between canonical and theological
approaches to ministry and orders were not perceived. Leo
therefore denied both orders and jurisdiction to the Church of
England, where the older theology could deny jurisdiction
without denying orders. Yet the theology of jurisdiction was
not more advanced in 1895 than it was in 1559. When
ARCIC-I stated in 1981, "Jurisdiction in the Church may be
defined as the authority or power (*potestas*) necessary for the
exercise of an office," it did not attempt to explain theologically
who has the power to give the office and the correlative
jurisdiction. There is still at this point a theological vacuum.
As long as it persists, doubt will be permitted as to the capacity
of one Church to pass judgment on the ministry of another;
and a shadow will remain on Leo XIII.

Steps and Stages

At the time of the Malta Report, it was foreseen by Bishop

Butler that the growing relations between Rome and Canterbury should pass through three stages.[21] Stage I was to be a doctrinal agreement, much of which was already reached. Stage II was to be nothing "short of 'intercommunion,' i.e. mutual authorization of what Roman Catholic theology calls *'communicatio in sacris'*, or participation in each other's liturgical prayer and sacraments." Stage III was to be "full communion." Bishop Butler was aware of many difficulties regarding stage II; and he acknowledged that several steps might be necessary to reach it. Twenty years later, after the completion of the *Final Report,* one should admit that the sequence of steps and stages is more complex than was implied in the three stages outlined by Bishop Butler. As proposed at the time, the passage to stage II would be assured by some supplemental regularization of orders.

There is merit in applying Ockham's razor to our question. One ought to prefer the simplest solution that is compatible with the complexity of the problem. Among the five ways to a solution that have been mentioned, the neatest and simplest is the first: recognition by presumption of validity. It would seem logically to follow from what Cardinal Willebrands' letter to the co-chairs of ARCIC-II envisaged as the next step in the growing relationships between the Roman Catholic and the Anglican Communions, namely, the endorsement of the *Final Report* as expressing the faith of Anglicans as well as Catholics regarding eucharist and orders.

The first way, however, should lead to the second. Once presumption of validity has been established, a further step will need to be taken. For a recognition of Anglican orders by the Catholic Church must still face the fact that orders are transmitted historically. A powerful objection is based upon this. For, granted that Paul IV had justifiable reasons to entertain a presumption of invalidity in regard to the Anglican episcopate, no later presumption of validity can retroactively restore the apostolic succession of bishops if this was interrupted by the assertion of the royal supremacy.

The solution of this dilemma lies in ecclesiology. In a *Communio*-ecclesiology, the *Ecclesia anglicana* did not cease to be the Church in England when it rejected papal primacy. And if it continued to be the Church, though in a state of schism

from both Rome and Constantinople, then it presumably preserved apostolic succession and the sixth sacrament, including
the fullness of it in its episcopate, canonical irregularities and
the tolerance of doctrinal divergences notwithstanding. The
point, once more, is not a question of defining the internal
essence of a sacrament; it is one of recognizing the ecclesial
horizon in which sacraments are administered. The fundamental recognition is not of orders, but of churchliness or
ecclesiality. As was envisioned in hope by Paul VI, the Catholic
Church of the West in communion with the bishop of Rome,
and the Churches of the Anglican Communion, have to become, or perhaps to discover that they are, Sister Churches.

At this point, however, a theological difficulty emerges from
Vatican Council II. When the Council distinguished, on the
one hand, between the Orthodox Church and the Churches
issued from the Reformation, and, on the other, between
"Churches and Ecclesial Communities," it took the eucharist
as the norm of discernment.[22] A Church is such because its
members are gathered around the eucharist, whereas an Ecclesial Community has no recognizable eucharistic center, although it may well have a recognizable baptism.

We thus arrive at the paradox that at one moment it is
ecclesiality or churchliness that is primordial and that enables
us to recognize the sacraments, and at another moment it is
the eucharist that is primordial and that enables us to recognize
the Church. There is in fact no way of escape from this dilemma. It is related to what modern theology calls a herme-
neutical circle: rules of interpretation are necessarily dependent
on the interpreter's position. Seen from within what one has
experienced as the Church, sacraments and orders are obvious
and need no other justification than their ecclesial setting. And
what has been experienced as the Church has been so experienced, as the Reformers would have said, in the preaching/
hearing of the Word and in the administration/reception of
the sacraments, central to which is the eucharist. This sends
us—not back, but forward—to what must be the consciousness
of being the Church in an ecclesiology of Communion. Paul
VI based the reflections of his first encyclical, *Ecclesiam suam*
(1964) on the consciousness of being the Church.[23] From this

consciousness there followed Pope Paul's insight that the structure of the Church is dialogical.

Hence the ultimate ecumenical perspective: it can only be in striving for mutual understanding and in progressively sharing the consciousness of being the Church, that Roman Catholics and Anglicans will heal the wounds caused in the body of Christ, at different times and different depths, by Thomas Cranmer's Ordinal and by Leo XIII's apostolic letter.[24]

Endnotes

Notes, Introduction

[1]*An Act concerning the Consecration of a Bishop.* See below, ch. 3, footnote 24.

[2]*Leonis Papae XIII Litterae Apostolicae De Ordinationibus Anglicanis,* Rome, 1896, p. 18 (n. 36, p. 22). I will refer to this as *Litt. Apost.;* the number and page in parenthesis will be from Canon Smith's English translation, *Anglican Orders-Still No Case,* London: Catholic Truth Society, 1946. In ordering the footnotes, one number will normally cover all quotations until the next footnote.

[3]l. c., p. 19 (n. 40, p. 23-24).

[4]Francis Clark's other major study examines the state of eucharistic doctrine on the eve of the Reformation: *Eucharistic Sacrifice and the Reformation,* Oxford: Blackwell, 1967.

[5]Giuseppe Rambaldi's articles are the following - In *Archivum Historiae Pantificiae:*
(1) *Una lettera del cardinale Richard sulla Fine della Revue Anglo-Romaine,* vol. 18, 1980, p. 403-410;
(2) *Leone XIII e la Memoria de L. Duchesne sulle Ordinazioni Anglicane,* vol. 19, 1981, p. 333-345;
(3) *Relazione et Voto del P. Raffaele Pierotti, Maestro del S. Palazzo Apostolico sulle Ordinazion Anglicane,* vol. 20, 1982, p. 337-338;
(4) *Un Documento Inedito sull'origine della Lettera di Leone XIII 'Ad Anglios,'* vol. 24, 1986, p. 405-414;
(5) *Verso l'incontro tra Catolici e Anglicani negli anni 1894-1896,* vol. 25, 1986, p. 405-410.
(6) In *Gregorianun: A proposito della Bolla Apostolicae Curae. Note di contesto e schemi preparatori,* vol. 61, 1980, p. 677-743;
(7) *La Memoria di L. Duchesne sulle Ordinazioni Anglicane,* vol. 62, 1981, p. 682-746;
(8) *La Bolla Apostolicae curae di Leone XIII sulle Ordinazioni Anglicane-I,* vol. 64, 1983, p. 631-637.
(9) *La Bolla Apostolicae Curae di Leone XIII sulle Ordinazioni Anglicane - II,* vol. 66, 1985, p. 53-88.
(10) *Il Voto del Padre Emilio De Augustinis sulle Ordinazioni Anglicane (1895),* vol., 50, 1981, p. 48-75. [I will abbreviate the reference by giving the name of the author and the number of the article: (1), (2), etc.]

Notes, Chapter 1

[1]Others presumably assisted Cranmer, but he was the main author. See W.H. Frere, *A New History of the Book of Common Prayer, with a Rationale of its Offices,* London: Macmillan, 3rd ed., 1955; Aidan Gasquet and Edmund Bishop, *Edward VI and the Book of Common Prayer,* London: Sheed and Ward, new ed., 1928; Edward P. Echlin, *The Anglican Eucharist in Ecumenical Perspective: Doctrine and Rite from Cranmer to Seabury,* New York: Seabury Press, 1968.

²Cranmer's writings will be quoted from *The Works of Thomas Cranmer* (Parker Society), 2 vol., Cambridge: University Press, 1844 and 1846.

³The first view was already common among the English Recusants of the 16th and 17th centuries; for the second view; see C.H. Smyth, *Cranmer and the Reformation under Edward VI,* Cambridge: University Press, 1926; C.W. Dugmore, *The Mass and the English Reformers,* London: Macmillan, 1958; Peter Brooks, *Thomas Cranmer's Doctrine of the Eucharist. An Essay in Historical Development,* New York: Seabury Press, 1965.

⁴George H. Tavard, *The Quest for Catholicity. The Development of High Church Anglicanism,* New York: Herder and Herder, 1963, p. 1-21 (citation, p. 20)

⁵*Works,* vol. 2, p. 113.

⁶*Works,* vol. 2, p. 114; see George H. Tavard, *Justification. An Ecumenical Study,* New York: Paulist, 1983, p. 67-69.

⁷*Works,* vol. 2, p. 150.

⁸The expression, *extra Calvinisticum,* designates the central thesis of Calvin's christology, that the risen Word of God is "outside" his body as well as "in" his body; it contradicts Luther's idea that the divine Word is nowhere but in his body, his body being everywhere by virtue of the divine attribute of immensity, in which it participates through the "communication of idioms."

⁹*Works,* vol. 1, p. 93.

¹⁰*Works,* vol. 1, p. 74.

¹¹*De eucharistia constanter credimus et docemus, quod in sacramento corporis et sanguinis domini vere, substantialiter, et realiter adsunt corpus et sanguis christi sub speciebus panis et vini (A Book containing Divers Articles . . .,* art. 7: *De Eucharistia,* in *Works,* vol. 2, p. 475.) It is possible that Cranmer did not work alone on these articles; he may have been assisted by more Catholic-minded bishops.

¹²See Tavard, *The Quest . . .,* p. 16-17.

¹³*Liturgies of King Edward VI* (Parker Society), Cambridge: University Press, 1844, p. 283.

¹⁴*Works,* vol. 2, p. 484-485. (The singular verb with the plural subject is in the text!)

¹⁵l. c., p. 485. Yet Cranmer did not believe that a liturgical ordination was absolutely necessary: appointment by the king was sufficient to make a bishop (*Questions and Answers concerning the Sacraments and the Appointment of Bishops and Priests,* 1540, especially questions 9 and 12 [*Works,* vol. 2, p. 116-117]).

¹⁶l. c., p. 486.

¹⁷l. c., p. 488-489.

¹⁸*De ministris ecclesiae docemus quod nemo debeat publice docere aut sacramenta ministrare, nisi rite vocatus, et quidem ab his penes quos in ecclesia, juxta verbum dei et leges ac consuetudines uniuscujusque regionis, jus est vocandi et admittendi (l. c., p. 477).*

¹⁹*Questions Put Concerning Some Abuses of the Mass, Works,* vol. 2, p. 151.

²⁰The text of the Ordinal is given in John Jay Hughes, *Stewards . . .,* p. 311-338, where the differences between the texts of 1550 and 1552 are indicated. I confess that my critique of *Stewards . . .* was excessive: see George H. Tavard, *Anglican Orders -Again (One in Christ,* 1971/1, p. 46-53), with the reply, John Jay Hughes, *Propter Unitatem (One in Christ,* 1971/2, p. 201-209).

²¹The findings of the colloquy were formulated in *The Regensburg Book,* the Latin

text of which, as edited by Melanchthon, is included in Melanchthon's works in *Corpus Reformatorum (Opera quae supersunt omnia,* vol. IV, Halle, 1837, p. 190-238); see George H. Tavard, *Holy Writ or Holy Church. The Crisis of the Protestant Reformation,* New York: Harper, 1959, p. 184-191. Ochino went to England later: Cranmer, always on the lookout for suitable scholars with Protestant leanings, invited him, along with Martin Bucer and Peter Martyr Vermigli.

22Text in Odoricus Raynaldus, *Annales ecclesiastici,* tome XIV, Lucca (Italy), 1738, p. 560-561.

Notes, Chapter 2

1Quoted in Florence Higham, *Catholic and Reformed. A Study of the Anglican Church, 1559-1662,* London: SPCK, 1962, p. 5; see similar quotations in V.J.K. Brook, *A Life of Archbishop Parker,* Oxford: Clarendon Press, 1962, p. 256-257.

2Text in David Wilkins, *Concilia Magna Britanniae et Hiberniae, ab anno MDXLVI ad annum MDCCXVII,* vol. 4, London, 1907, fol. 86.

3*Declaration against the Mass,* September 7, 1553, in *Works,* vol. 2, p. 429.

4*quid a nobis sperandum, quid tentandum, quid aut per nos aut quomodo agendum ac tractandum (Annales . . ..,* p. 498)

5*Annales . . . ,* p. 87.

6*perturbatum illic ac labefactatum purae Religionis cultum . . . pristinam Patrum disciplinam . . . In quo quid agere conveniat, tu quidem a nobis minime es admonendus, cui res illae aeque ac nobis ipsis corde sunt, et magis quam caeteris omnibus notae: illud quod nostrarum partium fuit, prompto et alacro animo fecimus, ut circumspectionem tuam amplissimis facultatibus a nobis atque ab hac Apostolica Sede muniremus per quas in errorem lapsos consolari, et in Dei gratiam ac Sanctae Catholicae Suae Ecclesiae communionem restituere possis, quemadmodum aliis nostris sub plumbo litteris, quas propediem ad te mittimus latius explicabitur (Annales . . ..,* p. 499).

7Joseph G. Dwyer, ed., *Pole's Defense of the Unity of the Church,* Westminster, Md: Newman Press, 1965.

8Eva-Maria Jung, *On the Nature of Evangelism in sixteenth-century Italy (Journal of the History of Ideas,* XIV/4, 1953, p. 511-527). The *Consilium de emendanda ecclesia* was composed of four cardinals (Catarini, Sadoleto, Carafa, and Pole), three bishops, one abbot (of San Giorgio in Venice), and the Dominican Thomas Badia, Master of the Sacred Palace. Some of its recommendations were anything but moderate: it recommended bringing all conventual religious orders to a slow death by forbidding them to take novices!

9W.H. Frere, *The Marian Reaction in its Relation to the English Clergy,* London: SPCK, 1896, p. 55-58.

10Ernest C. Messenger, *The Reformation, the Mass, and the Priesthood,* vol. 2, London: Longmans, Green and Co., 1937, p. 66.

11In the *Bulla facultatum extraordinarium,* of August 5, 1553, Julius III speaks of *bigamia . . ,* and refers to it further on as *heresim hujusmodi.* See Messenger, *Reformation . . ..,* vol. 2, p. 11; 28-30; Messenger, however, believes that *hujusmodi* designates Anglican heresies about the Mass.

12Frere, *Marian Reaction . . .,* p. 58-59.

[13]Wilkins, *Concilia* . . ., fol. 89.

[14]l. c., fol., 91.

[15]*quodque bigamia et irregularitate, ac aliis praemissis non obstantibus in eorum ordinibus, dummodo ante eorum lapsum in haeresim hujusmodi rite et legitime promoti vel ordinati fuissent* . . . (l. c.).

[16]*et non promoti ad omnes etiam sacros ordines ab eorum ordinariis* (l.c.).

[17]*qui matrimonium cum aliquibus virginibus, vel corruptis secularibus, etiam mulieribus, de facto eatenus contraxissent* . . . (l. c., fol. 92). *Mulieres* refers to married women.

[18]*etiam circa ordines, quos nunquam aut male susceperunt, et munus consecrationis, quod iis ab aliis episcopis vel archiepiscopis etiam haereticis et schismaticis, aut alias minus rite, et non servata forma ecclesiae consueta, impensum fuit* . . . (l. c., fol. 93).

[19]See below, ch. 3, footnotes 14 to 19.

[20]*Annales* . . ., p. 513.

[21]Messenger, *Reformation* . . ., vol. 2, p. 52.

Notes, Chapter 3

[1]*omni virtute praeditos* . . . *Praeclara charissimi* is printed in Frere, *Marian Reaction* . . ., appendix XIV, p. 223-232.

[2]*in earum matrimoniis sic contractis libere et licite remanere seu illa de novo contrahere* (l. c., p. 227).

[3]*ut in suis ordinibus et beneficiis remanere possent* (l. c.).

[4]*Ita tamen ut si qui ad ordines ecclesiasticos tam sacros quam non sacros ab alio quam episcopo aut archiepiscopo rite et recte ordinato promoti fuerunt, eosdemque ordines ab eorum ordinario de novo suscipere teneantur, nec interim in iisdem ordinibus ministrent* (l. c., p. 230).

[5]*gratiam et communionem apostolicae sedis* (Wilkins, *Concilia* . . ., fol. 129).

[6]*in forma ecclesiae consecratis et ordinatis, et propterea solum executione ordinis episcopalis carentibus* (l. c., fol. 140).

[7]*secundum eandem formam clericali charactere insignitus* (l.c.).

[8]*Regimini universalis ecclesiae* is in Frere, *Marian Reaction* . . ., p. 232-235: *ita tamen ut qui ad ordines tam sacros quam non sacros ab alio quam episcopo vel archiepiscopo rite et recte ordinato promoti fuissent eosdem ordines ab eorum ordinario de novo suscipere tenerentur, nec interim in ipsis ordinibus ministrarent* (p. 233).

[9]*quae diversas impetrationes, dispensationes, gratias, et indulta tam ordines quam beneficia ecclesiastica seu alias spirituales materias concernentia, praetensa auctoritate supremitatis ecclesiae Anglicanae nulliter et de facto obtinuerant* . . . (p. 233). These lines are quoted in *Apostolicae curae* without the word, *concernentia* (*Litt. Apost* . . ., p. 9 [n. 11, p. 11]). The word was in parliament's petition for the absolution from schism, though perhaps not in Pole's request for clarifications (as summed up in a document in the Vatican Archives). It was both in *Praeclara charissimi* and in *Requinimini universalis ecclesiae*. See the discussion of this omission in Messenger, *Reformation* . . . , vol. 2, 137-138; 141-144; Hughes, *Absolutely Null* . . . , 270, footnote 69. The issue is whether Paul IV declared various dispensations to be null (with the

word, *concernentia*), or the orders themselves to be null (without the word). With Hughes, I understand him to have declared the dispensations null, not the orders. Yet one cannot ascertain whether the omission of *concernentia* in the documentation that was placed at Leo's disposal was deliberate or accidental.

[10]Text as above, note 8 (p. 234).

[11]*schismate in ipso Regno vigente rite et recte ordinati dici possint* (1. c.).

[12]*qui schismate praecito durante ad ordines promoti fuerunt* (1. c.).

[13]*eos tantum episcopos et archiepiscopos, qui non in forma ecclesiae ordinati et consecrati fuerint, rite et recte ordinatos dici non posse, et propterea personas ab eis ad ordines ipsos promotas ordines non recepisse, sed eosdem ordines a suo ordinario juxta literarum nostrarum praedictarum continentiam et tenorem de novo suscipere debere et ad id teneri; alios vero quibus ordines husjusmodi collati fuerunt ab episcopis et archiepiscopis in forma ecclesiae ordinatis et consecratis, licet ipsi episcopi et archiepiscopi schismatici fuerint, et ecclesias quibus praefuerint de manu quondam Henrici VIII et Eduardi VI, praetensorum Angliae Regum, receperint, caracterem ordinum eis collatorum recepisse et executione ipsorum caruisse ...* (1.c.)

[14]*Summa Theologica, Suppl.,* g.37, a.2.

[15]*Ordinatur omnis ordo ad eucharistiae sacramentum,* 1. c., q. 40, a. 5.

[16]*... cum episcopus non habeat potestatem superiorem sacerdoti quantum ad hoc ...* (1. c.).

[17]1. c., q. 38, a. 2.

[18]1. c., q. 38, a. 2, ad 2.

[19]1. c., q. 38, a. 2. On the basis of St Thomas's theology, one could still hold that episcopal jurisdiction comes from Christ through the bishop of Rome, rather than from the bishop of Rome. The council of Trent refused to endorse the thesis of the papal origin of episcopal jurisdiction. This had been proposed by Jaime Laínez, the successor of St Ignatius at the head of the Society of Jesus.

[20]*sacramentum principaliter consistit in potestate tradita* (1. c., q. 34, a. 4).

[21]Bonaventure, *Commentary on the Sentences,* IV, d. 24, p. 1, a. 2, q. 2, ad 3.

[22]Denzinger-*Schönmetzer, Enchiridion Symbolorum,* n. 1326 (henceforth abbreviated as D.-Sch.)

[23]*Sextum sacramentum est ordinis, cujus materia est illud per cujus traditionem confertur ordo; sicut presbyteratus traditur per calicis cum vino et patinae cum pane porrectionem; diaconatus vero per libri evangeliorum dationem; subdiaconatus vero per calicis vacui cum patina vacua superposita traditionem; et similiter de aliis, per rerum ad ministeria sua pertinentium assignationem. Forma sacerdoti talis est: "Accipe potestatem offerendi sacrificium in ecclesia pro vivis et mortuis, in nomine Patris et Filii et Spiritus Sancti:" et sic de aliorum ordinum formis, prout in Pontificali Romano late continetur. Ordinarius minister hujus sacramenti est episcopus. Effectus augmentum gratiae, ut quis sit idoneus minister* (Wilkins, *Concilia ... , fol. 796).

[24]*An Act concerning the Consecration of a Bishop,* 1542, in Peter Kenrick, *The Validity of Anglican Ordinations and Anglican Claims to Apostolical Succession Examined,* Philadelphia, 1848, Appendix IV, p. 311-312.

Notes, Chapter 4

[1]See V.J.K. Brook, *A Life of Archbishop Parker,* Oxford: Clarendon Press, 1962.

[2]John Jewel, *Sermon preached at Paul's Cross*, in *The Works of John Jewel* (Parker Society), 4 vol., Cambridge, 1845-1850, vol. 1, p. 20. See John E. Booty, *John Jewel as Apologist for the Church of England*, London: SPCK, 1963.

[3]1. c., p. 21. There was a precedent for such a challenge in Cranmer's *Declaration against the Mass*, in the first weeks of Queen Mary's reign.

[4]On this literature, see A.C. Southern, *Elizabethan Recusant Prose, 1559-1582*, London: Sands and Co., 1950, p. 60-118. On Jewel and Harding, see Claire Cross, *The Royal Supremacy in the Elizabethan Church*, London: Allen and Unwin, 1969.

[5]Jewel, *Works*, vol. 3, p. 334.

[6]Quoted in Booty, 1. c., p. 75.

[7]1. c., p. 76.

[8]Jewel, *Works*, vol. 3, p. 320.

[9]Booty, 1. c., p. 66.

[10]Jewel, *Works*, vol. 3, p. 320.

[11]1. c., p. 321.

[12]1. c., p. 322.

[13]1. c., p. 336-337.

[14]Messenger, *Reformation . . .*, vol. 2, p. 368-369. See Marvin R. O'Connell, *Thomas Stapleton and the Counter Reformation*, New Haven: Yale University Press, 1964.

[15]Pedro de Ribadeneyra, *Historias de la Contrareforma*, Madrid: Biblioteca de Auctores Cristianos, 1945, p. 1069.

[16]1. c., p. 1087.

[17]1. c. p. 1083.

[18]1. c., p. 1086.

[19]*Regnans in excelsis* is printed in Jewel, *Works*, vol. 4, p. 1131-1132.

Notes, Chapter 5

[1]Donatism started with the denial, by several bishops, that the ordination of Cecilianus to the see of Carthage, in 312, was valid, and their consequent ordination of a rival, Majorinus, to whom Donatus soon succeeded. The reason given was that Cecilianus's chief consecrator had allegedly been a *traditor* (i.e., had surrendered the liturgical books) during the persecution of Diocletian, when he was a deacon in Carthage. The allegation was most probably false.

[2]The case of Pope Formosus is cited by Duchesne in his *Mémoire sur les ordinations anglicanes*, Rambaldi (7), p. 738-739; Duchesne mentions some other reordinations. On Hincmar, see George H. Tavard, *Episcopacy and Apostolic Succession according to Hincmar of Reims*, in *Theological Studies*, 34/4, December 1973, p. 594-623.

[3]Frere, *Marian Reaction . . .*; Messenger, *Reformation . . .*, vol. 2, p. 45-49.

[4]On the unnamed former Calvinist, see Messenger, 1. c., p. 465-481; Hughes, *Absolutely Null . . .*, p. 278-280. The important texts in the Vatican Archives are printed in S.M. Brandi, *La Condanna delle Ordinazioni Anglicane*, 4th ed., Rome, 1908 (serialized previously in *Civiltá Catolica*, 1896-1897).

[5]Messenger, l. c., p. 481-487; Hughes, l. c., p. 280-283; T.F. Taylor, *A Profest Papist. Bishop John Gordon,* London: SPCK, 1958.

[6]This text is reproduced in Kenrick, *Validity* . . ., appendix IV, p. 326-329.

[7]*Accipe potestatem praedicandi verbum Dei, et administrandi sancta ejus sacramenta.*

[8]Clement's decree was first published by Brandi (*Civiltá Catolica,* series XVI, vol. VIII, November 21, 1896, p. 433-434). An English translation is in Taylor, *Profest* . . ., p. 33-34. Meetings of the Holy Office on Thursday were considered more solemn than the regular weekly meetings, that would not be attended by the pope.

[9]Rambaldi (3), p. 374.

[10]The duchy of Lorraine not being part of the kingdom of France, Le Courayer's book did not need the king's licence to print. There were many other writings, that need not be considered here. Mason drew a refutation from a professor at Douai seminary, Anthony Champney (c. 1569-c.1643): *The Vocation of Bishops and other Ecclesiastical Ministers, proving the ministers of the pretended Reformed Churches in general to have no calling,* . . . *and in particular the pretended Bishops in England to be no true Bishops* (1616, with a Latin translation in 1618). Champney, however, weakened his case by holding the Nag's Head story to be true. Later in the century, Peter Talbot (1620-1680), future Catholic archbishop of Dublin, denied the validity of Anglican orders, in *The Nullity of the Prelatique Clergy and Church of England* (1659) and in his *Treatise of the Nature of Catholick Faith and Heresie* (1657). The distinguished Anglican theologian, John Bramhall (1594-1663) bishop of Derry, archbishop of Armagh, answered him in *Consecration and Succession of Protestant Bishops Justified* (1658). John Lewgar (1602-1665), who had been converted to Catholicism by William Chillingworth (1602-1644) in the years of Chillingworth's conversion to the Church of Rome (1630 to 1634), came out with two volumes. In *Erastus Junior* (1659) he demonstrated that Protestant and Anglican preachers had their authority to preach from the king only, not from Christ. He pursued the point in *Erastus Senior, scholastically demonstrating this conclusion, that (admitting the Lambeth records to be true) those called Bishops here in England are no Bishops, either in Order or in Jurisdiction, or so much as legal* (1662). An Anglican reply to Lewgar was by R.C. (possibly Ralph Cudworth), *A Scholastical Discourse* . . ., (London, 1663).

[11]See Norman Sykes, *Archbishop Wake,* London: Cambridge University Press, 1957; Edmond *Préclin, L'Union des Eglises gallicane et anglicane. Une tentative au temps de Louis XV: P.F. Le Courayer et Guillaume Wake,* Paris: Gamber, 1928.

[12]Messenger, *Reformation* . . . , vol. 2, p. 492. The correspondence between Archbishop Wake and two professors of the Sorbonne was published after the writing of the present book: Jacques Grés-Gayer, *Paris-Cantorbéry (1717-1720). Le dossier d'un premier oecuménisme,* Paris: Beauchesne, 1989. In his survey of the Thirty-nine Articles, Louis Ellies Dupin admits the validity of Anglican orders, while recognizing the possibility of a doubt, but he holds that the Gallican Church could lift the doubt by recognizing Anglican orders in an agreement of union (p. 200). Patrice Piers de Girardin bases his acceptance of Anglican orders on the method by which bishops are chosen in England, as reported to him by William Wake, that is, on a presumption of apostolic succession (p. 272).

[13]Aimé-Georges Martimort, *Le Gallicanisme de Bossuet,* Paris: Le Cerf, 1953; Georges Tavard, *La Tradition au XVIIe siècle en France et en Angleterre,* Paris: Le Cerf, 1969, p. 155-194.

[14]Quoted in Tavard, l. c., p. 169.

Notes, Chapter 6

[1]Messenger, *Reformation* . . , vol. 2, p. 508-601; Hughes's volume, *Absolutely Null* . . , remains indispensable for a study of the papal commission's work: although the Vatican Archives were not yet open for the period, the main lines of Hughes's analysis are vindicated by the archival documents that have been published by Rambaldi (see above, Introduction, footnote 5).

[2]Henry R.T. Brandreth, *Dr. Lee of Lambeth,* London: SPCK, 1951; Frederick George Lee (1832-1902) went further, and was involved in the creation of the Order of Corporate Reunion in 1877, by which time he had been uncanonically ordained a bishop in obscure circumstances, and he called himself bishop of Dorchester; in 1877, however, his wife Elvira was received in the Church of Rome; in December 1901, he was himself received in the Church of Rome, a few weeks before he died.

[3]The Latin texts are in *Acta Sanctae Sedis,* vol. 2, 1866: 1) *Supremae Sanctae Romanae et Universalis Inquisitionis Epistola ad Omnes Angliae Episcopos,* Sept. 16, 1864: p. 657-660; 2) letter from 198 Anglican clergy, no date: p. 660-662; and 3) the response of the Holy Office, addressed to *"Honorabiles et Dilectissimi Domini,"* Nov. 8, 1865: p. 662-668. The dossier includes a short introduction and a conclusion. The last two texts are given in English in a pamphlet by Edward Hanahoe, *Two Early Documents on Reunion,* Graymoor: Chair of Unity Octave, 1954.

[4]*Constitutio dogmatica 'Dei Filius',* D.-Sch., n. 3001-3020.

[5]Kenrick, *Validity* . . ., p. 177.

[6]Clark, *Anglican Orders* . . ., p. 26-32.

[7]Franzelin, who had been the main theologian at Vatican Council I, was the author of a *De Sacramentis in genere,* where the form of ordination was closely tied to the meaning of its terms: Messenger, *Reformation* . . ., vol. 2, p. 688-689. On the Abyssinian ordinations: Messenger, l. c., p. 734-742. Cardinal Patrizi's response is given in Latin and English in Arthur Lowndes, *Vindication of Anglican Orders,* 2, vol., New York: Gorham, 1911, vol. 2, appendix E, p. cccli-cccliii.

[8]Clark, l. c., p. 187.

[9]It is not necessary here to review all the literature that came out in 1894-1897. A number of authors joined the discussion as soon as it was known that Leo XIII was interested. Let us mention, against the validity, the English Jesuit, Sydney Smith (articles in *The Month,* 1894, and article, *Ordinations anglicanes,* in the French *Dictionnaire apologétique de la foi catholique,* vol. III, col. 1162-1228, Paris, 1916); for the validity, but with distinctive nuances, the French historian Auguste Boudinhon (first in a review of Dalbus, *Etude théologique sur les ordinations anglicanes* [in *Canoniste Contemporain,* June-July 1894], then in an essay, *De la Validité des ordinations anglicanes* [published in the same journal and also as a booklet, 1895]; Boudinhon's study is summed up in Messenger, *Reformation* . . ., p. 529-535).

[10]Rambaldi (7).

[11]Rambaldi (10).

[12]*Summa Theologica,* III, q. 64, a. 9, ad 1.

[13]Messenger, l. c., p. 567-569.

[14]The letters are in the dossier of the Vatican Archives, 10/5/1896 (English bishops), 1/5/1896 (Irish bishops), 3/5/1896 (Scottish bishops).

[15]Summaries, with quotations from Lacey, are given in Messenger, l. c., p. 557 ff.

[16]Hughes, *Absolutely Null* . . ., p. 180.

[17]Rambaldi (3).

[18]l. c., p. 376.

[19]1. c., p. 385.

[20]1. c., p. 388. This may be the source of the frequent, though not quite accurate, rendering of the formula of Leo XIII: "null and void."

[21]See above, footnote 3, and below, footnote 25.

[22]On "unionism", see Etienne Fouilloux, *Les Catholiques et l'unité chrétienne du XIXe au XXe siècle. Itinéraires européns d'expression française*, Paris: Le Centurion, 1982; George H. Tavard, *Two Centuries of Ecumenism*, Notre Dame: Fides, 1960.

[23]*Satis Cognitum. The Unity of the Church.* New York: Paulist, 1949, n. 33, p. 18.

[24]1. c., n. 55, p. 32.

[25]Hughes, *Absolutely Null . . .*, p. 81-91.

Notes, Chapter 7

[1]*In ritu cujuslibet sacramenti conficiendi et administrandi jure discernunt inter partem caeremonialem et partem essentialem quae materia et forma appellari consuevit. Omnesque norunt, sacramenta novae legis, utpote signa sensibilia atque gratiae invisibilis efficientia, debere gratiam et significare quam efficiunt et efficere quam significant. Quare significatio, etsi in toto ritu essentiali, in materia scilicet et forma, haberi debet, praecipue tamen ad formam pertinet; quum materia sit pars per se non determinata, quae per illam determinetur* (*Litt. Apost.*, p. 12-13 [n. 24, p. 16]). The text is very close to Mazzella's draft (Rambaldi [6], p. 715).

[2]*summum sacerdotium, sacri ministerii summa* (1. c., p. 13 [n.25, p. 17]); the quotation is from the council of Trent, session XXII, canon 3, (D.-Sch., no,. 1753).

[3]1. c., p. 14 (n. 39, p. 19: I have altered the translation: *summa* does not mean "summit", as Canon Smith has it!).

[4]*Lumen gentium*, n. 8.

[5]*. . . eo manifesto consilio ut alius inducatur ab Ecclesia non receptus, utque id repellatur quod facit Ecclesia et quod ex institutione Christi ad naturam attinet sacramenti* (*Litt. Apost.*, p. 17 [n. 33, p. 21]). For Leo XIII, the Anglican rite should signify, but does not, *ordinem sacerdotii vel ejus gratiam et potestatem, quae praecipue est potestas consecrandi et offerendi verum corpus et sanguinem Domini . . .* (1. c., p. 13 [n. 25, p. 16-17], with reference to council of Trent, session XXIII, can. 1, D.-Sch., n. 1771).

[6]This is a current problem too, in regard to the status of the Catholic Church in China: were the bishops who ordained other bishops without referring to Pius XII really free to do otherwise?

[7]*Unum quidem ex parte ejus qui profert verba, cujus intentio requiritur ad sacramentum, ut infra dicetur. Ei ideo, si intendat per hujusmodi additionem vel diminutionem alium ritum inducere qui non sit ab Ecclesia receptum, non videtur perfici sacramentum: quia non videtur quod intendat facere id quod facit Ecclesia (q. 64, a. 8).*

[8]Thomas Aquinas makes a distinction here. If the minister believes that baptism can be given in the name of the Virgin Mary, then *talis sensus esset contrarius verae fidei . . .* If, however, the name of the Virgin is added to the Trinity, in order to ask for her intercession, then this is not contrary to the faith and the baptism is valid. When he finds that *tolliatur debitus sensus verborum*, Aquinas concludes: *tollitur veritas sacramenti.*

[9]This was well put by the Recusant, Matthew Kellison, in 1629: "True it is that if you compare the power of order, by which the Priest can consecrate the bodie and

bloud of Christ and remitte sinnes, with the power the Bishop hath to consecrate Priests and other ministers, then the Priests power is greater, than is that which is proper to the Bishop; because the Bishop by the power to ordain ministers hath only power over *corpus Christi mysticum,* as divines saye, that is, over the Church; but the Priest by the power to consecrate the bodie and bloud of Christe hath power over *corpus Christi naturale,* the natural bodie of Christ, in that he by Christe his own words conuerteth breade into Christes bodie and wine into his bloud, and maketh them really present under the forme of breade and wine" (*A Treatise of the Hierarchie and Divers Orders of the Church against the Anarchie of Calvin,* Douai, 1629, reproduced as vol. 152 in the series, *English Recusant Literature, 1558-1640,* Menston, Yorks.: The Scholar Press, 1973).

[10]For a parallel between the Pontifical and the Ordinal, see Gasquet-Bishop, *Edward VI . . .,* p. 241-247.

[11]On the question of the "sacrificing priesthood," see the differing positions of Clark (*Eucharistic Sacrifice . . .*) and Hughes (*Stewards . . .,* p. 193-224.) For contemporary theological reflections, see Jean-Marie Tillard, *Sacrificial Terminology and the Eucharist* (in *One in Christ,* 1981/4, p. 306-323); George H. Tavard, *A Theology for Ministry,* Wilmington: Michael Glazier, 1983.

[12]On the Sarum rite of ordination, see Edward P. Echlin, *The Story of the Anglican Ministry,* Slough: St Paul Publications, 1974: quotation, p. 16; W.H. Frere, *The Use of Sarum. The Original Texts from the MSS,* Cambridge: University Press, 2 vol., 1898-1901 (vol. 2: *The Ordinal and tonal*).

[13]l. c., p. 7.

[14]l. c., p. 8.

[15]l. c., p. 10.

[16]l. c., p. 11.

[17]D.-Sch., n. 690; 700.

[18]The Articles are included in all editions of *The Book of Common Prayer* of the Episcopal Church, p. 603-611; see Giocondo Degano, *L'Episcopato nella Chiesa Anglicana. Un' Analisi delle Fonti Ufficiali,* Verona: Missioni Africane, 1974.

[19]D.-Sch., n. 856.

[20]*Conciliorum Oecumenicorum Decreta,* Basel:Herder, 1962, p. 503.

[21]*nativa Ordinalis indoles ac spiritus, uti loquuntur. . .* (*Litt. Apost.,* p. 15); Canon Smith's translation is not adequate: "The character and spirit of the Ordinal as it came into being . . ." (n. 31, p. 20). This "native character and spirit" is at the center of Cardinal Willebrands's letter on the "new context" for assessing Anglican orders: see next chapter.

[22]Clark, *Anglican Orders . . .,* p. 198.

[23]l. c., p. 199.

[24]l. c., p. 198.

[25]*Response of the Archbishops,* in Arthur Lowndes, *Vindication of Anglican Orders,* 2 vol., New Haven: Gorham, vol. 2, appendix B, p. cccxxxviii.

Notes, Chapter 8

[1]See chapter 7, footnote 25; the response is discussed, somewhat disingenuously, in Messenger, *Reformation . . .,* vol. 2, p. 590-596.

[2]n. XIX, in Lowndes, *Vindication . . .,* vol. 2, p. cccxxxii.

[3]l. c., p. cccxxxvi

[4]l. c., p. cccxxxviii.

[5]A summary is given in Messenger, l. c., vol. 2., p. 596-598.

[6]Published by F.X. Funk, *Didascalia et Constitutiones Apostolorum,* Paderborn, 1905; the text is cited by Kenrick, l. c., appendix XVI, p. 331; this appendix includes other ordination rites in patristic and medieval Pontificals.

[7]Gustave Delasges, *Validité des ordinations anglicanes,* Paris, 1895; Messenger does not seem to be acquainted with this book.

[8]Anthony Stephenson, *Anglican Orders,* Westminster, Md: Newman Press, 1956.

[9]Clark, *Anglican Orders . . . .,* p. 11-12.

[10]*Litt. Apost.,* p. 16 (n. 33, p. 21).

[11]Clark, l. c., p. 20.

[12]Rambaldi (10), p. 70-71.

[13]Clark, l. c., p. xiv.

[14]*Litt. Apost.,* p. 18 (n. 36, p. 22).

[15]D.-Sch., n. 110-111.

[16]On the letter to Cardinal Richard, see Rambaldi (1); Sydney Smith considers *Apostolicae curae* infallible because Leo XIII intended to settle the question once for all (*Dictionnaire apologétique . . .,* col. 1223-1224); Messenger objects that *Apostolicae curae,* though correct, cannot be infallible because it settles a point of discipline, not a dogmatic fact (*Reformation . . .,* vol. 2, appendix I, p. 733). As a point of discipline, Leo's decision could have been justified by simply pastoral reasons, as of prudence and sacramental "tutiorism." But the trend of the debate brought about a disproportion between Leo XIII's original concern and his eventual conclusion. Originally, the pope intended only to decide for or against the customary practice of absolute ordination for convert Anglican clergy who wished to function as priests in the Catholic Church. On this point, see A.F. von Gunten, *Les Ordinations anglicanes. Le problème affronté par Léon XIII (Nova et Vetera,* Jan.-March 1988, p. 1-21). But Leo soon tried to make a historical case for the practice, and to pass a historical judgment on events that were more than four hundred years old. Such a judgment necessarily remains open to on-going historical critique. An instance of overevaluation of science by a religious author, who himself was a historian, will be found in the life of the distinguished Quaker, Rufus Jones (1863-1949). His biographer tells us that in the course of his studies "he made necessary adjustments" to his beliefs and theories because he saw and knew then that the conclusions of science were not a series of happy guesses but instead were "inescapable facts about the universe verified by a multitude of workers and buttressed by unimpeachable testimony" (David Hinshaw, *Rufus Jones, Master Quaker,* New York: Putnam's Sons, 1951, p. 133). Contemporary scientists see their conclusions, not as inescapable facts, but only as successful hypotheses, that must be discarded when a better one is successfully tested. This applies, *mutandis mutatis,* to historical science.

[17]D.-Sch., n. 3095; *Lumen Gentium,* n. 25.

[18]*Litt. Apost.,* p. 17 (n. 35, p. 22). The translation has, "this point," instead of, "this point of discipline." A footnote by the translator identifies the Latin expression as *idem caput,* although "an earlier text appears to have read, *idem caput disciplinae."* An additional footnote by Messenger is more exact: "early editions" had the words *caput disciplinae,* but the "official text" in the *Acta Leonis XIII* of 1897 omitted the word *disciplinae* presumably on purpose. However, the text that I quote, of 1896, is no less official. One may surmise that the word *disciplinae* was dropped surreptitiously, by someone who may have been bribed . . . There have been other such cases in the history of the Vatican Press!

[19]In an address of September 7, 1955, Pius XII judged the bull *Unam sanctam* of Boniface VIII to be the fruit of Catholicism functioning as an "ideological system" that is not adequate to the Church; see George H. Tavard, *The Church, the Layman and the Modern World*, New York: Macmillan, 1959, p. 17-18; *The Bull 'Unam Sanctam' of Boniface VIII*, in Paul Empie and Austin Murphy, ed., *Papal Primacy and the Universal Church. Lutherans and Catholics in Dialogue, V*, Minneapolis: Augsburg, 1974, p. 105-119. Following Vatican Council II, Paul VI reformed the Missal, which Pius V had forbidden to alter (bull *Quo primum*, July 13, 1570). The Missal of Pius V had already been modified by Pius X, Pius XII and John XXIII! Another instance of a pope derogating to a disciplinary decision made by one of his predecessors would be the restoration of the Society of Jesus by Pius VII, in 1814, Clement XIV having declared the dissolution of the Society to be "inviolable in the future" [*in futurum inviolabiliter observari*] (brief *Dominus ac Redemptor*, June 21, 1773).

[20]*Unitatis redintegratio*, n. 13; the following quotation is from *Lumen gentium*, n.21.

[21]D.-Sch., n. 3858.

[22]1. c., n. 3859.

[23]1. c., n. 3860.

[24]In Paul VI's reform of the sacrament of orders, the "form" of ordination to the priesthood is: *Da, quaesumus, omnipotens Pater, his famulis tuis Presbyterii dignitatem; innova in visceribus eorum Spiritum sanctitatis; acceptum a te, Deus, secundi meriti munus obtineant, censuramque morum exemplo suae conversationis insinuent.* The "form" of ordination to the episcopate is: *Et nunc effunde super hunc Electum eam virtutem, quae a te est, Spiritum principalem, quem dedisti dilecto Filio tuo Jesu Christo, quem Ipse donavit sanctis Apostolis, qui constituerunt Ecclesiam per singula loca ut sanctuarium tuum, in gloriam et laudem indeficientem nominis tui* (*Documentation Catholique*, July 7, 1968, col. 1168-1169).

[25]Quoted in Robert Hale, *Canterbury and Rome, Sister Churches*, New York: Paulist, 1982, p. 16. On the notion of Sister Churches, see Emmanuel Lanne, *Eglises-soeurs. Implications ecclésiologiques du Tomos agapis (Istina*, 1975/1, Jan.-March, p. 47-74); *United Churches or Sister Churches: a Choice to be Made* (*One in Christ*, 1976/2, p. 106-123); Michael Fahey, *Ecclesiae Sorores ac Fratres: Sibling Communion in the Pre-Nicene Christian Era* (in *Proceedings of the Thirty-Sixth Annual Convention, Catholic Theological Society of America*, Cincinnati, Ohio, June 10-13, 1981, p. 15-38).

[26]Clark and Davey, 1. c., p. 112-113; ARCIC-I, *Final Report*, p. 114-115.

[27]*Final Report*, p. 5.

[28]1. c., p. 6.

[29]1. c., p. 38.

[30]1. c., p. 44-45. See the judgment of Archbishop Michael Ramsey on the effect of the Canterbury Statement, *Ministry and Ordination*, on the question of Anglican orders: "If priesthood is understood to be what the learned Roman Catholic, as well as Anglican, authors of the document say it is, then Pope Leo XIII will seem less right or wrong than irrelevant" (Michael Ramsey, *Canterbury Pilgrim*, New York: Seabury Press, 1974, p. 92).

[31]*Information Service of the Secretariat for Promoting Christian Unity*, n. 60, 1986 (I-II), p. 23. See Thomas Ryan, *Reflections on 'a New Context for Discussing Anglican Orders' (One in Christ*, 1986/3, p. 228-233). On May 8, 1990, the Anglican-Roman Catholic Consultation in the USA adopted an official statement entitled, *Anglican Orders: A Report on the Evolving Context of their Evaluation in the Roman*

Catholic Church. At the time of writing, this statement has been released to the public but has not yet been printed in the media.

[32] l. c., p. 24.

[33] l. c., n. 11, July 1970/III, p. 13.

[34] l. c., p. 14. See Emmanuel Lanne, *Pluralisme et unité: possibilité d'une diversité de typologies dans une même unité ecclésiale* (*Istina*, 1969/ 1, Jan.-March, p. 171-190). Lanne himself refers to Bernard Lambert, who, without elaborating the point, had spoken of a "typology of the forms of unity": *Le Problème oecuménique,* 2 vol., Paris: Le Centurion, 1962, vol. 1, p. 142-143. On the *Communio*-ecclesiology, see Jérôme Hamer, *L'Eglise est une Communion,* Paris: Le Cerf, 1962; Jean-Marie Tillard, *Eglise d'Eglises.* *L'ecclésiologie de communion,* Paris: Le Cerf, 1987; Willebrands, *Vatican II's Ecclesiology of Communion (One in Christ,* 1987/3, p. 179-191). The following reflection is pertinent here: "I am convinced that the method followed by Leo XIII's commission was bound to lead to a dead-end, for lack of an ecclesiology" (Jean-Marie Tillard, *Recognition of Ministries: What is the Real Question?* One in Christ, 1985/ 1, p. 31-39; citation, p. 36).

[35] *Commission Théologique Internationale. Textes et documents (1969-1985),* Paris: Le Cerf, 1988, p. 78.

[36] George H. Tavard, *Two Centuries of Ecumenism,* Notre Dame: Fides, 1960, p. 118.

[37] *La Documentation catholique,* n. 1469, April 17, 1966, col. 673, footnote 1.

Notes, Conclusion

[1] Christopher Butler, *Unity—an Approach by Stages?* (in Clark and Davey, l. c., p. 101-106; citation, p. 105).

[2] Liberius signed the first formula of Sirmium, of semi-Arian orientation (D.-Sch., n. 139-140), which ignored the doctrine of *homoousios* of the council of Nicaea. By endorsing the first council of Constantinople (381) as ecumenical, the council of Chalcedon (452) and all later bishops of Rome opposed the first firmula of Sirmium and pope Liberius. Vigil's orthodoxy was questioned in the West, because, while virtually a prisoner of Emperor Justinian in Constantinople (from 547 to 555), he agreed to the emperor's condemnation of "the three chapters." Honorius (pope, 625-538) agreed, without understanding the fine point of the question, that there is "one will" in Christ as there is one Person; later, Leo the Great (pope, 440-461) declared that Honorius had "consented to maculate the immaculate rule of apostolic tradition that he had received from his predecessors." On these cases, see Robert Eno, *Some Elements in the Pre-History of Papal Infallibility* (Paul Empie, Austin Murphy, and Joseph Burgess, ed., *Teaching Authority and Infallibility in the Church. Lutherans and Catholics in Dialogue, IV,* Minneapolis: Augsburg, 1980, p. 238-258).

[3] John XXII preached that the souls after death cannot enjoy the beatific vision until the last judgment and the resurrection of the flesh; this doctrine was declared heretical by his successor, Benedict XII (pope, 1334-1342).

[4] See above, chapter 8, footnote 19.

[5] Edward Yarnold, *Anglican Orders—a Way Forward,* London: Catholic Truth Society, 1977.

[6] In addition, Marco Antonio De Dominis (1566-1624), a former Jesuit who had been archbishop of Spalato from 1602 to 1616, before joining the Church of England, was a co-consecrator of George Montaigne (1569-1628) as bishop of Lincoln; dean of Windsor in 1617, he was expelled from England in 1622 for being involved in negotiations with the new pope, Gregory XV (1621-1623); he was taken back into the Catholic

Church, but was jailed by the Inquisition after the death of Gregory XV; he died in Castel San Angelo.

[7]By the principle of economy the Orthodox Church is able to discern the making of a true sacrament outside its own Communion, even when the conditions of ritual and doctrine are not adequate.

[8]Jean-Marie Tillard finds a basis for presumption of validity in the contribution of the ecclesial community to the transmission of orders: "There is no celebration outside the apostolic Tradition except in a situation of connivance between celebrant and assembly. This is why, it seems to me, the intention of causing a breach cannot be deduced simply on the basis of the ministers' doctrinal position . . . So if today, after a history during which the most traditional vision has ceaselessly resurfaced, the Anglican communion 'recognizes' in this vision its own faith, then it seems to me that it must be concluded that, in this case, the apostolic ministry has probably never been interrupted" (*Recognition . . .*, p. 37-38).

[9]California-ARC: mimeographed documentation.

[10]Jean-Marie Tillard, *Le 'votum ecclesiae', L'eucharistie dans la rencontre des chrétiens*, in *Miscellanea Liturgica in onore di S. E. il Card. G. Lercaro*, Paris: Desclée, 1967, vol. 2., p. 143-194. Elsewhere, Tillard remarks: "Faced with a breach of this continuity (of succession by the laying on of hands), the broadest solution, for cases within the Catholic community, is a *sanatio in radice* . . .," whereas the common practice for those outside the Catholic community is (re)ordination, which is usually absolute rather than conditional (*Recognition . . .*, p. 31). That *sanatio in radice* might replace (re)ordination is an intriguing hypothesis, though somewhat hazardous, as it presupposes a capacity in the bishop of Rome that Anglicans may be reluctant to acknowledge.

[11]See *Eucharist and Ministry. Lutherans and Catholics in Dialogue, IV*, Washington: USCC Publications Office, 1970, p. 31-32.

[12]l. c., papers on apostolic succession by James McCue (p. 138-171) and Walter Burghardt (p. 173-177).

[13]l. c., p. 33.

[14]Butler, in Clark and Davey, l. c., p. 105.

[15]I have written from time to time on the question: George H. Tavard, *The Recognition of Ministry* (*Journal of Ecumenical Studies*, vol. 5/4, 1967, p. 629-649); *Roman Catholic Theology and Recognition of Ministry* (*Journal of Ecumenical Studies*, vol. 6/4, 1968, p. 623-628; reprinted in *Eucharist and Ministry, Lutherans and Catholics in Dialogue, IV*, p. 301-305); *The Recognition of Ministry (Journal of Ecumenical Studies*, vol. 11/1, 1974, p. 65-84); *The Recognition of Ministry: What is the Priority? (One in Christ*, 1987/1-2, p. 21-35).

[16]*Baptism, Eucharist and Ministry*, Geneva: World Council of Churches, 1982, p. 32.

[17]*The Recognition of Ministry*, l. c., 1974, p. 67.

[18]Kellison, *A Treatise . . .*, p. 180.

[19]Kellison, l. c., p. 174-175.

[20]Decree on the Sacrament of Orders, session XXIII, July 15, 1563, canon 7 (D.-Sch., n. 1777); see n. 1769.

[21]Butler, l. c., 103-106.

[22]See *Lumen gentium*, n. 15; *Unitatis redintegratio*, n. 13-18.

[23]*Ecclesiam suam. First Encyclical Letter, Pope Paul VI,* Washington: NCWC, 1964, n. 18-40, p. 8-18; see my oral remarks in: *"Ecclesiam suam." Première Lettre Encyclique de Paul VI (Colloque International,* Rome, 24-26, October 1980), Brescia: Istituto Paolo VI, p. 170-171.

[24]In his inaugural address at the second session of Vatican II (1963), Paul VI set the example of repentance for the sins against other Christians committed by Catholics in the name of the Church (Hans Küng, Yves Congar, Daniel O'Hanlon, *Council Speeches of Vatican II,* New York: Paulist, 1964, p. 146). The council incorporated this attitude in the decree *Unitatis redintegratio,* n. 7.

Index